TWO WITNESSES
AT GETTYSBURG

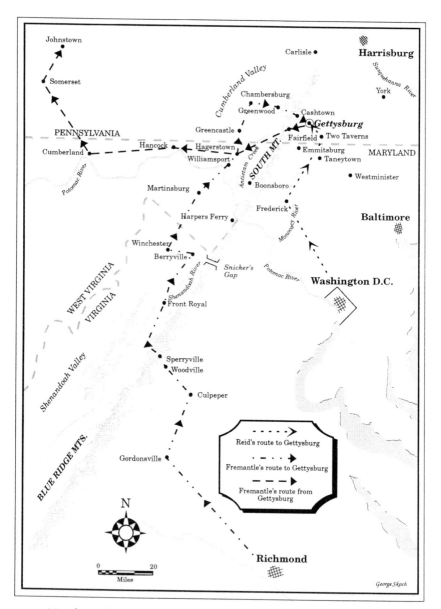

Northern Virginia and Southern Pennsylvania, with routes to
Gettysburg of Reid and Fremantle

TWO WITNESSES AT GETTYSBURG:

The Personal Accounts of Whitelaw Reid and A. J. L. Fremantle

Edited by
Gary W. Gallagher

BRANDYWINE PRESS • St. James, New York

ISBN 1-881089-11-8

1st Printing 1994

Telephone Orders: 1-800-345-1776

Printed in the United States of America

For Barnes F. Lathrop,
whose example as a scholar always will remain with me

Table of Contents

Introduction

"Pennsylvania invaded! Harrisburg expected to fall! Lee's whole army moving through Chambersburg in three columns of attack!" In these words, written at Philadelphia on June 19, 1863, Whitelaw Reid began his coverage of the Gettysburg campaign for readers of the Cincinnati *Gazette*. Eleven days later Reid was in Washington, D.C., making final preparations to join the Union Army of the Potomac as it marched northward to strike the rebel force in southern Pennsylvania. When Reid wrote his initial article, Arthur James Lyon Fremantle, a British visitor to America, watched events closely from the Confederate capital of Richmond, Virginia. Eager to observe what promised to be a major confrontation between the two most famous armies of the Civil War, Fremantle decided to attempt a rendezvous with the Army of Northern Virginia as it maneuvered on northern soil. Both men soon found themselves on the battlefield at Gettysburg, witnessed action on the second and third days of fighting, and wrote accounts that offer modern readers a wealth of anecdotes and insights about the largest and bloodiest battle ever fought in the Western Hemisphere.

Born near Xenia, Ohio, on October 27, 1837, Reid had spent a childhood surrounded by books and music. A somewhat frail boy, he read voraciously, did well in school, and attended Miami University of Ohio, where he graduated with honors in 1856. Reid embraced the Republican party and the antislavery cause while a university student, supporting Republican presidential candidate John C. Frémont in 1856. Four years later he worked for the nomination of Abraham

Lincoln. By the time of Lincoln's election, Reid had labored several years as a journalist in Xenia and elsewhere. Hired by the editor of Cincinnati's *Gazette* to cover Ohio troops serving in western Virginia after the outbreak of war in 1861, Reid displayed talent as a reporter from the field. His radical Republican politics conformed to the editorial stance of the *Gazette,* and his dispatches, signed "Agate" (perhaps because of Reid's fondness for the quartz stones), won a wide audience. His stories about military operations in the war's western theater—and especially a classic narrative of the battle of Shiloh—won him promotion in June 1862 to the post of Washington correspondent for the *Gazette.* It was in that capacity that he wrote his gripping account of Gettysburg.[1]

Reid's reporting benefited from his study of military history, but A. J. L. Fremantle had the advantage of professional experience as a soldier. He was born in November 1835, the first son of Major General John Fremantle, a distinguished British officer of the early 19th Century. Young Fremantle entered the army in 1852 and a year later received a position in the Coldstream Guards, a much-honored unit in which his father also had served. By 1860, though only twenty-five years old, he had been promoted to captain in the Coldstream Guards and lieutenant colonel in the British Army. Posted to Gibraltar that year, he followed news from America with interest.[2] Fremantle initially favored the North because of his own antislavery sympathies, but came to identify with southerners in their struggle against long odds. A meeting in January 1862 with Confederate naval captain Raphael Semmes, whom Fremantle conducted on a tour around Gibraltar,

[1] This brief sketch of Reid's background is drawn from Bingham Duncan, *Whitelaw Reid: Journalist, Politician, Diplomat* (Athens, Ga.: University of Georgia Press, 1975), chapters 1–2; James G. Smart's introduction to *A Radical View: The 'Agate' Dispatches of Whitelaw Reid, 1861–1865,* 2 vols. (Memphis, Tenn.: Memphis State University Press, 1976); and Allan Nevins's sketch of Reid in Allen Johnson and Dumas Malone, eds., *Dictionary of American Biography,* 20 vols. and index (New York: Charles Scribner's Sons, 1928–37), 15:482–86.

[2] For a summary of Fremantle's professional life, see his obituary in the *Times* of London, September 26, 1901.

deepened the Englishman's respect for the South.[3] Fifteen months later Fremantle stepped off a vessel near the mouth of the Rio Grande River to begin a memorable journey across the Confederacy. Traveling through Texas and seven other Confederate states en route to Virginia, he met a number of military and political luminaries and observed daily life in the embattled nation. He kept a diary along the way in which he wrote about people, events, and sights. The entries for June 20–July 15 detail Fremantle's activities during Lee's raid into Pennsylvania.

Because he arrived at Gettysburg too late to see the first day's fight, Reid relied on testimony from various participants to construct his narrative of the opening phase of the action. He succeeded in collecting much pertinent detail and went a long way toward explaining Confederate success on July 1 in stating that the "enemy was concentrating faster than we. Perhaps no one was to blame for it. . . ." The arrival of two divisions of Richard S. Ewell's Second Corps north of Gettysburg that afternoon *had* tipped the balance in favor of the Confederate forces, obliging first O. O. Howard's Eleventh Corps and then John F. Reynolds's First Corps to retreat to high ground south of Gettysburg. Unlike many others who have written about Gettysburg, Reid credits Howard's corps, which counted thousands of Germans among its ranks, with stout resistance against the initial southern assaults. He does accuse the corps of losing all formation once in Gettysburg, however, and of breaking in "wild confusion" in its haste to reach the safety of Cemetery Hill and other high ground—charges that would cloud the reputation of Howard's soldiers for many decades thereafter.[4]

Reid's coverage of the second and third days conveys the

[3] On Fremantle's meeting with Semmes, see Raphael Semmes, *Memoirs of Service Afloat, During the War Between the States* (Baltimore: Kelly, Piet and Company, 1869), p. 315.

[4] The quotations are on pages 34–35 below. A concise account of the first day's battle is Warren W. Hassler, Jr., *Crisis at the Crossroads: The First Day at Gettysburg* (University, Ala.: University of Alabama Press, 1970).

tension among Federal officers as Lee's infantry and artillery hammered at both of Meade's flanks. Shifting troops to meet successive crises at the Wheatfield, Little Round Top, and Culp's Hill on July 2, Meade managed to stave off defeat by the slimmest of margins. Reid experienced the Confederate bombardment of Cemetery Ridge that preceded the assault by Pickett and Pettigrew on July 3, describing in vivid language that trauma and the Union repulse of what he terms Lee's "last desperate attack." The southern offensive amounted to "fruitless sacrifice," he concludes: "They gathered up their broken fragments, formed their lines, and slowly marched away."[5]

Fremantle accords less attention than Reid to the details of the fighting, yet some of his vignettes are among the most quoted in all the military literature on the Civil War. A pair of these concern James Longstreet and R. E. Lee on the afternoon of July 3. Unaware that the Pickett-Pettigrew assault already had failed, Fremantle rode up to Longstreet as the survivors of the attack streamed back toward Seminary Ridge from Cemetery Ridge. Believing he had arrived in time to see the assault launched, Fremantle said to Longstreet, *"I wouldn't have missed this for any thing." "The devil you wouldn't!"* replied Longstreet with grim humor. *"I would like to have missed it very much; we've attacked and been repulsed: look there!"* A short time later Fremantle came upon Lee, who was rallying Confederate soldiers. An officer who approached Lee to complain about the condition of his troops heard his commander respond soothingly, "Never mind, General, *all this has been* MY *fault*—it is *I* that have lost this fight, and you must help me out of it in the best way you can." Fremantle thus preserved for readers an instance of

---

[5] The quotations are on pages 68 and 73 below. Two masterful books that analyze the fighting on July 2 are Harry W. Pfanz's *Gettysburg—The Second Day* (Chapel Hill, N.C.: University of North Carolina Press, 1987) and *Gettysburg—Culp's Hill and Cemetery Hill* (Chapel Hill, N.C.: University of North Carolina Press, 1993).

Lee's willingness, uncommon among Civil War commanders, to shoulder full responsibility for his actions.[6]
    Several prominent officers receive special attention from Reid and Fremantle. Sharing a common political outlook with O. O. Howard, Reid at several points in his dispatches includes admiring comments about the "brave, one-armed, Christian fighting hero." His description of Meade on July 1, when he first saw the Army of the Potomac's chief, is splendid, as is his crisp paragraph about the wounded Daniel E. Sickles on the morning of July 3. The "grim and stoical" Sickles, gamely puffing on a cigar despite the loss of a leg the previous day, fairly defines military courage. At his best in passages about Lee and Longstreet, Fremantle also furnishes sharp snapshots of an obviously ill A. P. Hill on July 1, the flamboyant George E. Pickett and J. E. B. "Jeb" Stuart, and the rather "remarkable-looking old soldier," Richard S. Ewell, during the army's retreat toward the Potomac River.[7]
    Small incidents punctuate the larger story of the battle in both accounts, reminding readers that any large event consists of innumerable small ones. One of Reid's best scenes concerns his fellow newspaper correspondent Samuel Wilkeson, who struggled to maintain his journalist's composure on July 2 while worrying about his son, an artillerist who had been wounded on July 1 (Wilkeson would find out later that his son was dead).[8] Fremantle mentions that during a bom-

---

[6] The quotations are on pages 127 and 130 below. On the assault by Pickett and Pettigrew, see George R. Stewart, *Pickett's Charge: A Micro-history of the Final Attack at Gettysburg* (Boston: Houghton Mifflin, 1959) and chapter 19 of Edwin B. Coddington, *The Gettysburg Campaign: A Study in Command* (New York: Charles Scribner's Sons, 1968). Coddington's magisterial work remains the best single-volume treatment of the campaign.
    [7] The quotations are on pages 37, 57, and 138 below.
    [8] For additional information on Wilkeson and other journalists mentioned by Reid, see J. Cutler Andrews, *The North Reports the Civil War* (Pittsburgh, Pa.: University of Pittsburgh Press, 1955), Emmet Crozier, *Yankee Reporters, 1861–65* (New York: Oxford University Press, 1956), and Louis M. Starr, *Bohemian Brigade: Civil War Newsmen in*

bardment on July 2 a Confederate band played polkas and waltzes—"which sounded very curious, accompanied by the hissing and bursting of the shells." He also relates that Lee, in the midst of trying on July 3 to bring order to the broken units of Pickett's division, stopped to reproach an officer who was whipping a horse frightened by the explosion of an artillery shell.[9] Modern readers who conceive of Gettysburg as a decisive Union victory that shattered Confederate morale should pay heed to Reid and Fremantle. Although Reid notes that "For once the Army of the Potomac had won a clean, honest, acknowledged victory," he closes with three paragraphs betraying his unhappiness that Lee's force had escaped across the Potomac. His last image is not of a victorious Union army but of officers squabbling, rumors of Meade's resignation, and a lethargic pursuit of the retreating Confederate troops. Fremantle marveled at the high morale among many rebel soldiers immediately after the Pickett-Pettigrew assault. As he prepared to depart for England eleven days later, he scoffed at northerners who insisted that Lee now led a broken command: "All this sounded very absurd to me, who had left Lee's army four days previously as full of fight as ever— much stronger in numbers, and ten times more efficient in every military point of view, than it was *when it crossed the Potomac to invade Maryland a year ago.*"[10] Other evidence sustains Reid and Fremantle. The impact of the battle on the armies, as well as on civilians North and South, was far more complex than usually is imagined.

A reluctance of many northerners to sacrifice for the Union stands out in Reid's early pages. He alludes to Pennsylvania men who rush to telegraph offices to spread alarm

---

Action (New York: Alfred A. Knopf, 1954). Each of these titles underscores Reid's reputation for being one of the best northern war correspondents.

[9] The quotation is on page 123 below.

[10] The quotations are on pages 73 and 158 below.

about the rebels but do not join the army. A regiment from New England that had enlisted for nine months and refused to remain in the field to help defeat Lee comes in for harsh criticism, as do swarms of Union stragglers who have left their commands to prey on civilians along the path of the army. Reid prescribes "Death on the spot" for stragglers. Fremantle also mentions lukewarm support for the Union among German-speaking civilians in Pennsylvania: "They are the most unpatriotic people I ever saw, and openly state that they don't care which side wins, provided they are left alone." Fremantle's account of anti-draft rioting that broke out in New York City shortly after Gettysburg alerts readers to a telling instance of unhappiness with the Union war effort.[11]

The riot expressed the racism that pervaded 19th-Century American society, and Fremantle's diary suggests some of the difficulties black people faced on both sides of the Potomac. Early on, one southern soldier informs the Englishman matter-of-factly that before the war "we were a lazy set of devils; our niggers worked for us, and none of us ever dreamt of walking, though we all rode a great deal." In the New York City of the riot, states Fremantle, no "colored man or woman was visible or safe in the streets, or even in his own dwelling." He ascribes much of this sentiment in the North to fear of economic competition from black workers. The poorer whites who could not pay the $300 necessary to avoid

---

[11] The quotations are on pages 16 and 108 below. Many soldiers in both armies commented about what they perceived as selfishness on the part of German–Americans (usually referred to as Pennsylvania Dutch) in southern Pennsylvania. Typical was Brig. Gen. Alpheus S. Williams, who wrote on June 30: "The inhabitants are Dutch descendants and quite Dutch in language ... the people are rich, but ignorant of everybody and [every]thing beyond their small spheres. They have immense barns, looking like great arsenals or public institutions, full of small windows and painted showily. Altogether, they are a people of barns, not brains." Alpheus S. Williams, *From the Cannon's Mouth: The Civil War Letters of General Alpheus S. Williams*, ed. Milo M. Quaife (Detroit: Wayne State University Press and the Detroit Historical Society, 1959), p. 224.

the draft "naturally hate being forced to fight in order to liberate the very race who they are most anxious should be slaves."[12] Fremantle's own ethnic and class prejudices surface occasionally in his diary. An English officer and gentleman, he felt most comfortable around upper-class southerners who, with an eye toward the help they might receive if Britain recognized the Confederacy, almost certainly went out of their way to make their guest welcome. He sees the men who served Confederate generals as "gentlemen of position and education, who have now been trained into excellent and zealous staff officers." In contrast, he dismisses a former northern streetcar driver as a "vulgar, ignorant, and low-born Federal officer" and expresses vast amusement at the sight of a slave who had exchanged clothes with a white Union soldier. Although he professes antislavery views in the preface to his published diary, Fremantle apparently accepted Confederate arguments that slaves were happy in bondage. He insists that most black men in the South would fight for their masters—though he warns of the consequences of rousing the passions of black men and "allowing them free scope."[13]

Apart from the violence in New York and a modest

---

[12] The quotations are on pages 90 and 160 below. Fremantle's allusion to $300 concerns the northern policy of commutation, which allowed draftees to pay a $300 fee (approximately a half-year's wages for a worker) to avoid conscription. In both North and South, draftees also had the option of hiring a substitute to serve for them. In July 1864, the United States Congress abolished commutation, after which the price of substitutes shot up. In December 1863, the Confederate Congress did away with substitution and made eligible for the draft all those who had purchased substitutes. On the subject of antipathy toward black Americans among white northerners, see V. Jacque Voegeli, *Free but Not Equal: The Midwest and the Negro during the Civil War* (Chicago: University of Chicago Press, 1967), and Forrest G. Wood, *Black Scare: The Racist Response to Emancipation and Reconstruction* (Berkeley and Los Angeles: University of California Press, 1970).

[13] The quotations are on pages 92, 103, and 142 below.

amount of Confederate plundering in Pennsylvania, Fremantle found the North physically untouched by the war. Reid spoke of near-panic in Frederick, Maryland, and of wildly shifting moods in Washington, D.C., as Lee's army marched north. Not the presence of Confederate invaders but the threat of them triggered these reactions. Fremantle noted the large number of military-age men in civilian clothes in Philadelphia and New York, the apparent wealth of many people on the streets, and the productive farms that dominated the northern countryside. These impressions were strikingly at odds with those he had recorded before crossing the Potomac. The area around Sperryville, Virginia, was "completely cleaned out" after suffering two years of campaigning armies: "It is almost uncultivated, and no animals are grazing where there used to be hundreds. All fences have been destroyed, and numberless farms burnt, the chimneys alone left standing. It is difficult to depict and impossible to exaggerate the sufferings which this part of Virginia has undergone."[14] Here and elsewhere Fremantle lays to rest the notion that hard war came to the Confederacy only with Ulysses S. Grant and William Tecumseh Sherman in 1864. Readers of these parts of the diary will come to see that deciding whether northerners or Confederates were more devoted to the struggle requires considering which population was more tested.

Reid continued to work as a journalist throughout the war, covering, among other stories, the fall of Richmond and Lincoln's funeral. He traveled extensively in the South after Appomattox and lived in Louisiana and Alabama for a time before returning to the North.[15] In 1868, the same year he published a massive study of Ohio during the Civil War, he went to work for Horace Greeley at the New York *Tribune*.[16]

[14] The quotation is on page 87 below.

[15] Reid recorded his observations about the defeated South in *After the War: A Southern Tour* (Cincinnati and New York: Moore, Wilstach and Baldwin, 1866).

[16] Reid titled his book *Ohio in the War: Her Statesmen, Her Generals, and Soldiers*, 2 vols. (Cincinnati and New York: Moore, Wilstach

Becoming editor of the *Tribune* shortly after Greeley's death in 1872, Reid brought modern methods of production to the paper and wielded considerable national influence. President Benjamin Harrison named him minister to France in 1889, and in 1892 he ran unsuccessfully as the vice-presidential candidate on the Republican ticket with Harrison. Six years later President William McKinley placed Reid on the commission that negotiated peace following the war with Spain; in 1905, Theodore Roosevelt named him ambassador to Great Britain, an appointment renewed by William Howard Taft when he succeeded Roosevelt in the White House. Reid died in London on December 15, 1912. His remains, carried across the Atlantic on a British warship, were subsequently buried in Tarrytown, New York.[17]

Fremantle's later career followed a comparably distinguished path. Returning to England in the summer of 1863, he published the portion of his diary devoted to Lee's Pennsylvania campaign in *Blackwood's Magazine*. The next year the first English printing of the entire diary appeared under the title *Three Months in the Southern States: April–June 1863*. American publishers North and South quickly followed with their own editions.[18] Confederates understand-

---

and Baldwin, 1868). The first volume deals principally with Ohio politics, the second with military topics.

   [17] See *Making Peace with Spain: The Diary of Whitelaw Reid, Sept.–Dec. 1898*, ed. H. Wayne Morgan (Austin, Tex.: University of Texas Press, 1965), for Reid's service on the peace commission. Chapters 15–16 of Duncan, *Whitelaw Reid*, discuss Reid as ambassador to Great Britain.

   [18] The September 1863 issue of *Blackwood's Magazine* carried the excerpt of Fremantle's diary; W. Blackwood and Sons of Edinburgh and London published the initial English edition of the complete work. The first American publishers, John Bradburn of New York and S. H. Goetzel of Mobile, Alabama, brought out their editions in 1864. Goetzel used wallpaper wrappers because by that point in the war paper was difficult to obtain in the Confederacy. Two other versions of the book merit mention. In *The Fremantle Diary: Being the Journal of Lieutenant Colonel James Arthur Lyon Fremantle, Coldstream Guards, on His Three Months in the South-*

ably praised the book, which depicted their cause as a gallant resistance to a brutal foe, while later generations of writers quoted from it frequently. It rapidly won a reputation as one of the best foreign commentaries on the conflict—a view still prevalent among students of the Civil War.[19] Fremantle remained in the British army, advancing to the rank of major general in 1882 and holding a number of commands before being named governor of Malta in 1894, a post he held for five years. He died on September 25, 1901, at the headquarters for the Royal Yacht Squadron.[20]

Whitelaw Reid and A. J. L. Fremantle bequeathed a substantial legacy to anyone interested in the Gettysburg campaign. Their accounts, which nicely complement each other, summon the past in a way possible only with firsthand observations. Modern readers who traverse the pages that follow have the opportunity to form, from the same texts read by thousands of Americans during the Civil War, their impressions of Gettysburg and the events surrounding it. They will see why it is important to review as much eyewitness testimony as possible in attempting to reconstruct any episode from the past. There is no one "truth" or single set of facts to be learned from history. Many truths emerge from the writings of witnesses who see different aspects of the same event

---

ern States (Boston: Little, Brown, 1954), Walter Lord made a number of editorial changes (including reversing Fremantle's first two names). The first paperback edition was a facsimile of Bradburn's 1864 printing, published by the University of Nebraska Press (Lincoln, Nebraska, 1991).

[19] For representative comments about the value of Fremantle's diary, see Douglas Southall Freeman, *The South to Posterity: An Introduction to the Writing of Confederate History* (New York: Charles Scribner's Sons, 1939), p. 19; Allan Nevins and others, eds., *Civil War Books: A Critical Bibliography*, 2 vols. (Baton Rouge, La.: Louisiana State University Press, 1967, 1969), 1:91; and Richard B. Harwell, *In Tall Cotton: The 200 Most Important Confederate Books for the Reader, Researcher, and Collector* (Austin, Tex.: Jenkins Publishing Company, 1978), p. 22.

[20] Fremantle's later life is outlined in his obituary in the *Times* of London, September 26, 1901.

or who perceive the same phenomenon in divergent ways. Often conflicting and sometimes irreconcilable, testimony from participants demonstrates that there are no easy answers to historical questions and no one interpretation about an event such as Gettysburg that will satisfy everyone.

Gary W. Gallagher
Pennsylvania State University

Acknowledgments

I am delighted to express thanks to several people whose help made the preparation of this small book possible. Professor James G. Smart of Keene State College kindly permitted me to use his edition of Whitelaw Reid's "Agate" dispatches relating to Gettysburg. Professor Smart also generously agreed to my changing a few spellings of proper names to bring Reid's text into conformity with Fremantle's. James Kirby Martin of the University of Houston first raised the possibility of this project, and his powers of persuasion eventually led me to take on what turned out to be a very pleasant project. George F. Skoch, who serves as cartographer for many a Civil War author, prepared the maps. Finally, David Burner of Brandywine Press proved to be an ideal publisher—generous, enthusiastic, and genuinely interested in my ideas about how to shape the book.

Editorial Note

The text of Whitelaw Reid's "Agate" dispatches relating to Gettysburg is taken from James G. Smart, ed., *A Radical View: The 'Agate' Dispatches of Whitelaw Reid, 1861–1865,* 2 vols. (Memphis, Tenn.: Memphis State University Press), 2:1–69. The text of A. J. L. Fremantle's diary covering the period from June 20 to July 15, 1863, comes from the 1864 edition of *Three Months in the Southern States: April–June 1863* published in New York by John Bradburn. To avoid confusion, I silently changed spellings of proper names so they appear the same in both accounts and corrected a few misspellings of other words. Otherwise, the texts have not been changed. The notes identify people mentioned by Reid and Fremantle, explain military terms, offer context for some events, and point readers toward material pertinent to various subjects. The maps and illustrations were added to permit readers to match images to text, and the appendix is designed to assist anyone unfamiliar with the command structure and ranks in Civil War armies.

Whitelaw Reid

I

THE GETTYSBURG CAMPAIGN

A Contemporary Account by Whitelaw Reid

ASSIGNMENT

1863, June 18
From Philadelphia

"Pennsylvania invaded!" "Harrisburg expected to fall!" "Lee's whole army moving through Chambersburg in three grand columns of attack!" And so on for quantity.

Such were the pleasing assurances that began to burst on us in the West on Tuesday morning. All Pennsylvania seemed to be quivering in spasms over the invasion. Pittsburgh suspended business and went to fortifying; veracious gentlemen along the railroad lines and in little villages of the interior rushed to the telegraph offices and did their duty to their country by giving their fears to the wings of the lightning. . . .

I was quietly settling myself in comfortable quarters at the Neil House to look on at the counterpart of last week's Vallandigham Convention[1] when dispatches reached me,

---

[1] Reid's reference is to the Ohio state Democratic convention, which convened in Columbus on June 11 and nominated Clement L. Vallandigham for the governorship. A leader of the northern Peace Democrats (often called Copperheads), Vallandigham had been arrested for treason on May 5, 1863, and, following banishment to Confederate lines, took up exile in Canada that July. The peace movement in the North gained thousands of adherents in the spring of 1863.

urging an immediate departure for the scene of action. I was well convinced that the whole affair was an immense panic, but the unquestioned movements of Lee and Hooker gave certain promise to something; and besides, whether grounded or groundless, the alarm of invasion was a subject that demanded attention.[2] And so, swallowing my disgust at the irregular and unauthorized demonstrations of the rebels, I hastened off.

A hasty trunk packing and a rush to the depot; and while the delegates to the great Union Convention were gathering by thousands and crowding Columbus as Columbus had never of late been crowded before, save when the people rushed spontaneously to arms at the first call for volunteers, the train was off for Pittsburgh and the East.[3]

RUMORS

1863, June 24
From Washington

Washington has become the most *blasé* of cities. She has been "in danger" so long that to be out of danger would give her an unnatural, not to say unpleasant shock.

Just now the indications warrant greater apprehension here than at any point throughout the North; rebel papers incautiously admit that Lee has set out for the capture of Washington and the subjugation of Maryland. The disposi-

[2] Gen. R. E. Lee's Army of Northern Virginia and Maj. Gen. Joseph Hooker's Army of the Potomac had begun to move north during the second week in June. The two armies had been watching each other warily along the Rappahannock River since the Confederate victory at Chancellorsville on May 1–4, 1863.

[3] The Union Convention met in Columbus the week after the Democrats gathered, and Republican party leaders secured the gubernatorial nomination of a former Democrat named John Brough. Running against the absent Vallandigham, Brough won the election by a margin of 100,000 votes.

tion of Hooker's forces seems to warrant the inference that he takes the same view of the rebel plans, and at any rate the whole rebel army is but a short distance from us, and adverse fortunes in the daily expected battle might leave us comparatively at their mercy; yet Harrisburg, Pittsburgh, and even Philadelphia, are frantic, if compared with the unruffled serenity of the Capital. Being in danger pays, and besides, it isn't so very unpleasant a sensation, when you get used to it. . . .

The bulk of Lee's army is still believed to be lying on the west side of Blue Ridge, in the vicinity of Snicker's Gap. Either army is protected in front from the other by the mountain, and matters look very much as if they had reached a deadlock. Some unexpected movement may of course precipitate a collision any hour; or Lee may suddenly dash off on some invading movement that will leave Hooker with a long stern chase before him; but on the other hand there is nothing to make it look improbable that we may have comparative inaction for a month.

While we hold Harper's Ferry and one or two other important points in the neighborhood, an invasion of Southern Pennsylvania is difficult, if not impossible. Lee cannot attack Hooker in front, without forcing the Blue Ridge gaps; if he attempts to ascend the valley and come out on Hooker's flank, he exposes himself on a long flank march, and leaves his transportation and supplies in a hazardous position. Altogether, it begins to look very much as if he had been checkmated in his grand movement of invasion. But,—it is never wise to exult too soon.

1863, June 28
From Washington

I have just returned from a flying visit to Frederick, Maryland. . . .

On the streets of the old fashioned Maryland town I met

General Seth Williams,[4] broad faced and genial looking as ever, though the stumpy red beard has sadly changed the familiar appearance of the workingman of McClellan's staff in the earlier days of the war. He had just made fifty miles without leaving the saddle!

From two such instances the movement can be inferred. The energy has been amazing, the rapidity of movement unprecedented in the East, and equaled only by such dashing operations in the West as Mitchel's advance into Alabama....[5]

The week, it would seem, must bring a battle; two days may do it. Our fates depend on no *one* battle now; but if a good Providence shall at last turn the scale in our favor, it will be a sorrier day for rebeldom than defeat of theirs on any field has hitherto proved.

THE BATTLES OF GETTYSBURG

[Our space this morning is largely occupied with the details of the great battles fought Wednesday, Thursday and Friday of last week, near Gettysburg, Pennsylvania. These reports are from the pen of our well known correspondent Agate, who was on the field, and witnessed all that it was possible for one man to see. As a descriptive writer Agate has few equals, and in addition, he has a merited reputation for reliability that adds largely to the value of his correspondence. We have no space this morning for more than this

---

[4] Brig. Gen. Seth Williams, a native of Maine, served as adjutant general of the Army of the Potomac during the period of the Gettysburg campaign. The adjutant general operated as the primary administrative aid to the commanding general.

[5] Reid probably had in mind the advance into Alabama of Federal troops under the command of Brig. Gen. Ormsby MacKnight Mitchel, which had resulted in the capture of Huntsville and Decatur on April 11–13, 1862.

brief reference to the reports which we spread before our readers.—Cincinnati *Gazette,* July 8, 1863]

Washington, June 29, 1863

Getting a Good Ready

"Would like you (if you feel able) to equip yourself with horse and outfit, put substitutes in your place in the office, and join Hooker's army in time for the fighting."

It was a dispatch, Sunday evening, from the manager, kindly alluding to a temporary debility that grew out of too much leisure on a recent visit west. Of course, I felt able, or knew I should by tomorrow. But, alas! it was Hooker's army no longer. Washington was all a-buzz with the removal. A few idol worshippers hissed their exultation at the constructive disgrace; but for the most part, there was astonishment at the unprecedented act and indignation at the one cause to which all attributed it. Any reader who chanced to remember a few paragraphs in a recent number of the *Gazette,* alluding to the real responsibility for the invasion, must have known at once that the cause was—Halleck.[6] How the cause worked, how they quarrelled about holding Harper's Ferry, how Hooker was relieved in consequence, and how, within an hour afterward, Halleck stultified himself by telling Hooker's successor to do as he pleased concerning this very point, all this will be in print long before this letter can get west.

For once Washington forgot its *blasé* air, and through a few hours there was a genuine, old-fashioned excitement. The two or three Congressmen who happened to be in town were indignant, and scarcely tried to conceal it; the crowds talked over the strange affair in all its phases; a thousand

---

[6] Maj. Gen. Henry Wager Halleck of New York, general-in-chief of the Union armies.

false stories were put in circulation, the basest of which, per-haps, was that Hooker had been relieved for a fortnight's continuous drunkenness; rumors of other charges, as usual, came darkening the very air.

Never before in the history of modern warfare had there been such a case. A General had brought his army by brilliant forced marches face to face with the enemy. They were at the very crisis of the campaign; a great battle, perhaps the battle of the war, was daily if not hourly impending. No fault of generalship was alleged, but it happened that a parlor chief-tain in his quiet study three score miles from the hourly-changing field, differed in judgment on a single point from the General at the head of the troops. The latter carefully examined anew the point in issue, again satisfied himself, and insisted on his conviction, or on relief from responsibility for a course he felt assured was utterly wrong. For this he was relieved—and within five hours was vindicated by his suc-cessor.[7]

But a good, perhaps a better general was put in his place—except from the unfortunate timing of the change, we had good reason to hope it would work, at least no harm. There was little regret for Hooker personally; it was only the national sense of fair play that was outraged.

Presently there came new excitement. Stuart[8] had crossed the Potomac, twenty-five miles from Washington, had captured a train within twelve or thirteen miles, had thrown out small parties to within a mile or two of the rail-road between Baltimore and Washington. In the night the road would certainly be cut, and for a few hours at any rate the Capital isolated from the country. We had need to make haste, or it might be difficult "to join Hooker's army."

---

[7] For a much less flattering view of Hooker's generalship in the opening phase of the Gettysburg campaign, see Edwin B. Coddington, *The Gettysburg Campaign: A Study in Command* (New York: Charles Scribner's Sons, 1968), pp. 635–36 n.118.

[8] Maj. Gen. James Ewell Brown "Jeb" Stuart, a Virginian who com-manded the cavalry in the Army of Northern Virginia.

Maj. Gen. Joseph Hooker

It was not to be a solitary trip. Samuel Wilkeson, the well-known brilliant writer on the New York *Tribune,* lately transferred to the *Times;* and Uriah H. Painter, chief Washington correspondent of the Philadelphia *Inquirer,* a miracle of energy in such a sphere, were to go; and C. C. Coffin of the Boston *Journal,* known through all New England as "Carleton," had telegraphed an appointment to meet me in the army.[9]

Monday morning Washington breathed freer on learning that the Baltimore trains had come through. Stuart had failed, then? But we counted too fast.

A few hasty purchases to make up an outfit for campaigning along the border, and at eleven we were off. Unusual vigilance at the little blockhouses and embankments at exposed points along the road; soldiers out in unusual force, and every thing ready for instant attack; much chattering of Stuart and his failure in the train; anxious inquiries by brokers as to whether communication with New York was to be severed; and so we reach Baltimore.

"Am very sorry, gentlemen; would get you out at once if I could; would gladly run up an extra train for you; but—the rebels cut our road last night, this side of Frederick, and we have no idea when we can run again." Thus Mr. Prescott Smith,[10] whom every body knows, that has ever heard of the Baltimore and Ohio Railroad.

---

[9] Reid's three companions were among the more prominent northern newspaper correspondents of the war. Samuel Wilkeson, a New Yorker and former lawyer, initially headed the Washington bureau of the New York *Tribune* and during the Gettysburg campaign held the same post for the New York *Times*. A young Quaker from West Chester, Pennsylvania, Uriah Hunt Painter of the Philadelphia *Inquirer* was notable for his close working relationship with Secretary of War Edwin M. Stanton. Charles Carleton Coffin, a native of New Hampshire, remained an army correspondent throughout the war and subsequently published a number of books about the conflict and delivered more than 2,000 lectures about his exploits.

[10] William Prescott Smith was the Master of Transportation for the Baltimore and Ohio Railroad, with headquarters in Baltimore.

And so Stuart had *not* failed—we were just one train too late and were cut off from the army! There was nothing for it but to wait; and so—ill satisfied with this "Getting a Good Ready"—back to Washington.

Off

Frederick, Md., Tuesday evening, June 30.

Washington was again like a city besieged as after Bull Run. All night long troops were marching; orderlies with clanking sabres clattering along the streets; trains of wagons grinding over the bouldered avenue; commissaries were hurrying up their supplies; the quartermaster's department was like a beehive; every thing was motion and hurry. From the War Department came all manner of exciting statements; men were everywhere asking what the President thought of the emergency. Trains had again come through regularly from Baltimore, but how long could it continue? Had not Stuart's cavalry been as near as the old Blair place at Silver Springs,[11] and might they not cut the track any moment they chose? Might they not, indeed, asked the startled bankers, might they not indeed charge past the forts on the Maryland side, pay a hurried visit to the President and Cabinet, and replenish their army chests from *our* well-stored vaults?

In the midst of all this there came a blistering sight that should blacken evermore every name concerned. With cries for reinforcements from the weakened front, with calls for volunteers and raw militia to step into the imminent breach and defend the invaded North, with everywhere urgent need for every man who knew how to handle a musket, there came sprucely marching down the avenue, in all their freshness of

[11] Francis Preston Blair, Sr., a close adviser to President Andrew Jackson whose son Montgomery served as Lincoln's postmaster general, called his country estate near Washington "Silver Spring."

brilliant uniforms and unstained arms, with faultlessly appareled officers and gorgeous drum major and clanging band and all the pomp and circumstance of glorious war (about the Capital,) with banners waving and bayonets gleaming in the morning sunlight, as with solid tramp that told of months of drill they moved down the street—in such bravery of peaceful soldiering there came a New England nine months' regiment, mustering over nine hundred bayonets, whose term of service that day expired! With Stuart's cavalry swarming about the very gates of the Capital, with the battle that was to decide whether the war should henceforth be fought on Northern or Southern soil hourly impending, these men, in all the blazonry of banners and music and glittering uniforms and polished arms, were marching—home! They had been implored to stay a fortnight, a week—three days even; but with one accord they insisted on starting *home*! Would that Stuart *could* capture a train that bears them!

Another exciting ride over a yet unmolested track, and we are again in Baltimore. Mr. Prescott Smith gave us the cheering assurance that the road was open again to Frederick; that nobody knew where Stuart had gone, but that in any event they would send us out in the afternoon.

For the rest there was news of more dashing movements by our army. The rebels were reported concentrating at York, Pennsylvania. Our army had already left Frederick far in the rear, and spreading out like a fan to make use of every available road, it was sweeping splendidly up to meet them. There was no fear of their not fighting under Meade. He was recognized as a soldier, brave and able, and they would follow him just as readily as Hooker—some of them indeed, far more willingly. But there was sore need for every musket. Lee at least equalled us in numbers, they thought.[12]

Baltimore had been in a panic. Monday evening some

[12] Maj. Gen. George Gordon Meade inherited an Army of the Potomac from Hooker that would number slightly fewer than 90,000 men at Gettysburg; Lee's army would bring approximately 70,000 men to the field.

rebel cavalry had ventured up to within a few miles of the city, and frightened persons had rushed in with the story that great squadrons of horse were just ready to charge down the streets. Alarm bells rang, the Loyal Leagues[13] rushed to arms, the thoroughfares were thronged with the improvised soldiery, and within an hour thousands of bayonets guarded every approach. It was worthy the new life of Baltimore. Here, thank God, was an eastern city able and ready at all times to defend itself.

Stuart did not come—if he had, he would have been repulsed.

General Erastus B. Tyler[14] (former Colonel of the Seventh Ohio) had been hastily summoned here to assume command of the defences of Baltimore. This display of citizen soldiery was part of the work he had already done.

But those "defences!" "Small boy," exclaimed Wilkeson as we sauntered through the street and passed an urchin picking pebbles out of a tar barrel to fling at a passing pig, "small boy," and he uttered it with impressive dignity, "You must stop that, sir! You are destroying the defences of Baltimore!" And indeed he was. Single rows of tar barrels and sugar hogsheads, half filled with gravel, and placed across the streets with sometimes a rail or two on top, after the fashion of a "stake and rider" fence, constituted the "defences." They were called barricades, I believe, in some official paper on the subject. Outside the city, however, were earthworks, (to which additions had been made in the press of the emergency,) that would have afforded considerable resistance to

---

[13] In response to rising antiwar sentiment among elements of the Democratic party, a group of business and professional leaders had created the Union League and Loyal Publication Society in 1862. The Loyal Leagues and Union Leagues functioned as an adjunct of the Republican party, disseminating literature supporting the war effort and attacking Democrats who questioned the Lincoln administration's policies. Republicans called themselves the Union party for much of the war.

[14] Brig. Gen. Erastus Barnard Tyler, born in New York and reared in Ohio.

an attack; and if cavalry had succeeded in getting into the city, the "barricades" might have been of some service in checking their charges.

In the afternoon Stuart's cavalry was heard from, making the best of its way by a circuitous route on the rear and flank of our army, to join Lee in Southern Pennsylvania. Baltimore, then, was safe; and Stuart had made the most ill advised raid of the war. He had worn out his horses by a terrible march on the eve of a desperate battle when, in the event of a retreat, he was especially needed to protect the rear and hold our pursuit in check; and in return he had gained—a few horses, a single army train which he could only destroy, eighteen hours' interruption of communications by rail between the Capital and the army, and night's alarm in Washington and Baltimore.

Our own army was now reported to be concentrating at Westminster, manifestly to march on York. To reach this point, we must take the Western Maryland road, but this had been abandoned in terror by the Company, and the rolling stock was all in Philadelphia. There was nothing for it but to hasten to Frederick, then mount and follow the track of the army.

As our party stepped into the train a despatch brought Hooker's vindication as against Halleck. He had been relieved for insisting on withdrawing the troops from Harper's Ferry and using them in the active operations of the army. Precisely that thing his successor had done! All honor to Meade for the courage that took the responsibility!

It was a curious ride up the road. Eighteen hours ago the rebels had swarmed across it. The public had no knowledge that they were not yet in its immediate vicinity and might not attack the very train now starting; yet here were cars crowded to overflowing with citizens and their wives and daughters willing to take the risks rather than lose a train. Mr. Smith had been good enough to provide a car for our party, but the press was so great we had to throw open the

Samuel Wilkeson

doors to make room for women and children, recklessly ready to brave what they supposed the dangers of the ride.

Frederick is Pandemonium. Somebody has blundered frightfully; the town is full of stragglers, and the liquor-shops are in full blast. Just under my window scores of drunken soldiers are making night hideous; all over the town they are trying to steal horses or sneak into unwatched private residences or are filling the air with the blasphemy of their drunken brawls. The worst elements of a great army are here in their worst condition; its cowards, its thieves, its sneaks, its bullying vagabonds, all inflamed with whiskey, and drunk as well with their freedom from accustomed restraint.

The Rear of a Great Army

Two Taverns P. O., Pa., July 1.

Our little party broke up unceremoniously. Both my companions thought it better to go back to Baltimore and up to Westminster by rail on the expected Government trains; I thought differently and adhered to the original plan of proceeding overland. I have already good reasons to felicitate myself on the lucky decision.

An hour after breakfast sufficed for buying a horse and getting him equipped for the campaign.

Drunken soldiers were still staggering about the streets, looking for a last drink or a horse to steal, before commencing to straggle along the road, when a messenger for one of the New York papers, who had come down with despatches, and myself were off for headquarters. We supposed them to be at Westminster but were not certain.

South Mountain, historic evermore, since a previous rebel invasion faded out thence to Antietam, loomed up on the left amid the morning mists;[15] before us stretched a wind-

---

[15] A Federal victory at South Mountain on September 14, 1862, set the stage for the battle of Antietam three days later.

ing turnpike, upheaved and bent about by a billowy country that in its cultivation and improvements began to give evidence of proximity to Pennsylvania farmers. The army had moved up the valley of the Monocacy through Walkersville, Woodbury, and Middleburg—all pleasant little Maryland villages—where in peaceful times Rip Van Winkle might have slumbered undisturbed. The direction seemed too far north for Westminster, and a courier, coming back with despatches, presently informed us that headquarters were not there but at Taneytown, a point considerably farther north and west. Evidently there was a change in our plans. We were not going to York, or headquarters would not be at Taneytown; and it was fair to suppose that our movements to the northwest were based upon news of a similar concentration by the rebels. The probabilities of a speedy battle were thus immensely increased, and we hastened the more rapidly on.

From Frederick out the whole road was lined with stragglers. I have heard General Marsena R. Patrick highly spoken of as an efficient Provost-Marshal General for the Potomac Army; but if he is responsible for permitting such scenes as were witnessed today in the rear, his successor is sadly needed.[16]

Take a worthless vagabond, who has enlisted for thirteen dollars a month instead of patriotism, who falls out of ranks because he is a coward and wants to avoid the battle, or because he is lazy and wants to steal a horse to ride on instead of marching, or because he is rapacious and wants to sneak about farmhouses and frighten or wheedle timid countrywomen into giving him better food and lodging than camp life affords—make this armed coward or sneak or thief

[16] Brig. Gen. Marsena Rudolph Patrick, a New Yorker, served as provost marshal general of the Army of the Potomac through most of the war. For his description of problems of straggling and poor discipline during the 1863 Pennsylvania campaign, see chapter 8 of *Inside Lincoln's Army: The Diary of General Marsena Rudolph Patrick, Provost Marshal General, Army of the Potomac,* ed. David S. Sparks (New York: Thomas Yoseloff, 1964).

drunk on bad whiskey, give him scores and hundreds of armed companions as desperate and drunken as himself—turn loose this motley crew, muskets and revolvers in hand into a rich country with quiet, peaceful inhabitants, all unfamiliar with armies and army ways—let them swagger and bully as cowards and vagabonds always do, steal or openly plunder as such thieves always will—and then, if you can imagine the state of things this would produce, you have the condition of the country in the rear of our own army on our own soil today.

Of course these scoundrels are not types of the army. The good soldiers never straggle—these men are the *debris,* the offscourings from nearly a hundred thousand soldiers.

There is no need for permitting these outrages. An efficient Provost Marshal, such as General Patrick has been called, would have put a provost guard at the rear of every division, if not of every regiment and brigade, and would have swept up every man that dared to sneak out of ranks when his comrades were marching to meet the enemy. The rebels manage these things better. Death on the spot is said to be their punishment for straggling, and in the main it is a just one.

The army itself had done surprisingly little damage to property along their route. Breaking off the limbs of cherry trees to pick the ripe cherries seemed to be about the worst of their trespasses. I have never before seen the country so little injured along the line of march of a great army.

But every farmhouse was now filled with drunken loafers in uniform; they swarmed about the stables, stealing horses at every opportunity and compelling farmers to keep up a constant watch; in the fence corners groups of them lay, too drunk to get on at all.

As we neared the army a new phase of the evil was developed. A few mounted patrols seemed to have been sent out to gather up the stragglers, and some of them had begun their duty by getting drunk, too.

In one fence corner we passed a drunken trio in fierce altercation with a gay-looking, drunken patrol with a rose jauntily worn in his button-hole and a loaded and cocked revolver carelessly playing in his hand. "These fellows are d-dr-drunk," he explained to us, "and ac'ly talk about sh-shootin' me for or'rin 'em to go to camp." One of the stragglers had his musket cocked and handsomely covering the red rose on the patrol's breast.

A few yards further on was another drunken party under the trees. A patrol, trying to get them started, was just drunk enough to be indiscreetly brave and talkative. "You're cowardly stragglers, every rascal of you," he roared, after a few minutes' unavailing efforts of coaxing. "You're lyin' scoune'rl," was the thick-tongued response; and the last we saw of the party as we galloped on, two of the stragglers were rushing at the patrol, and he was standing at a charge, bayonets ready to receive them. They probably halted before they reached the bayonet point.

As we stopped at a farmhouse by the roadside to feed our horses and get dinner, we passed a party of stragglers in the yard. After dinner to our amazement we discovered that my luckless "rebel look"[17] and an indignant reply about straggling to some impertinent question they had asked, had well-nigh got us into trouble. The rascals, drunk enough to half believe what they said, and angry enough at being called stragglers to do us any mischief they were able, had held a court on our cases while we were eating, had adjudged us rebel spies and had sentenced us to—have our horses confiscated! Luckily my companion strolled down to the stable after dinner just as the fellows were getting the horses out to make off with them! They announced their conclusion that we were spies, and their sentence, and insisted on the horses, but a judicious display of hearty disposition on his part to

---

[17] Reid wore his hair long in what was considered a "southern style."

knock somebody down induced them to drop the reins and allow him to put the horses back in the stable.

We had small time, as we galloped through, to appreciate the beauties of Taneytown, a pleasant little Maryland hamlet, named in honor of the Chief Justice of the United States (who has a countryseat in the vicinity,)[18] and like him now somewhat fallen into the sere and yellow leaf. Army trains blocked up the streets; a group of quartermasters and commissaries were bustling about the principal corner; across on the hills and along the road to the left, far as the eye could reach, rose the glitter from the swaying points of bayonets as with steady tramp the columns of our Second and Third corps were marching northward. They were just getting started—it was already well on in the afternoon. Clearly something was in the wind.

Half a mile further east, splashed by the hoofs of eager gallopers, a large, unpretending camp, looking very much like that of a battalion of cavalry—we turn in without ceremony and are at the headquarters of the Army of the Potomac.

At first all seems quiet enough, but a moment's observation shows signs of movement. The slender baggage is all packed, everybody is ready to take the saddle at a moment's notice. Engineers are busy with their maps; couriers are coming in with reports; the trustiest counsellors on the staff are with the General.

In a plain little wall tent, just like the rest, pen in hand, seated on a camp-stool and bending over a map, is the new "General Commanding" for the Army of the Potomac. Tall, slender, not ungainly, but certainly not handsome or graceful, thin-faced, with grizzled beard and moustache, a broad and high but retreating forehead, from each corner of which the slightly-curling hair recedes, as if giving premonition of baldness—apparently between forty-five and fifty years

---

[18] Roger Brooke Taney of Maryland, author of the majority opinion in the famous Dred Scott case, served as chief justice of the United States from 1836 until his death in October 1864.

of age—altogether a man who impresses you rather as a thoughtful student than a dashing soldier—so General Meade looks in his tent.

"I tell you, I think a great deal of that fine fellow Meade," I chanced to hear the President say a few days after Chancellorsville. Here was the result of that good opinion. There is every reason to hope that the events of the next few days will justify it.

A horseman gallops up and hastily dismounts. It is a familiar face—Lorenzo L. Crounse,[19] the well-known chief correspondent of the *New York Times* with the Army of the Potomac. As we exchange hurried salutations, he tells us that he has just returned from a little post village in Southern Pennsylvania, ten or fifteen miles away; that a fight, of what magnitude he cannot say, is now going on near Gettysburg between the First corps and some unknown force of the enemy; that Major General John F. Reynolds[20] is already killed, and that there are rumors of more bad news.

Mount and spur for Gettysburg is, of course, the word. Crounse, who is going too, acts as guide. We shall precede headquarters but a little. A few minutes in the Taneytown tavern porch, writing despatches to be forthwith sent back by special messenger to the telegraph office at Frederick; then in among the moving mass of soldiers and down the Gettysburg road at such speed as we may. We have made twenty-seven miles over rough roads already today; as the sun is dipping in the woods of the western hilltops, we have fifteen more ahead of us.

It is hard work, forcing our way among the moving masses of infantry, or even through the crowded trains, and

[19] Lorenzo Livingston Crounse, who grew up on the Wisconsin frontier, reported on the war for a number of western newspapers and the New York *World* before covering the Army of the Potomac for the New York *Times*.

[20] Maj. Gen. John Fulton Reynolds, a Pennsylvanian, operated as a wing commander in charge of the First, Third, and Eleventh corps of the Army of the Potomac between June 25 and his death on July 1.

Maj. Gen. George Gordon Meade

we make but slow progress. Presently aids and orderlies begin to come back, with an occasional quartermaster or surgeon or commissary in search of stores. Crounse seems to know every body in the army, and from every one he demands the news from the front. "Everything splendid; have driven them five or six miles from Gettysburg." "Badly cut up, sir, and falling back." "Men rushed in like tigers after Reynolds's death, and swept everything before them." (Rushing in like tigers is a stock performance, and appears much oftener in the newspapers than on the field.) "Gettysburg burnt down by the rebels." "Things were all going wild, but Major General Winfield S. Hancock got up before we were utterly defeated,[21] and I guess there's some chance now." "D--d Dutchmen of the Eleventh corps broke and ran like sheep, just as they did at Chancellorsville, and it's going to be another disaster of just the same sort."[22] "We still hold Gettysburg, and everything looks favorable." "Major General James S. Wadsworth's division cut to pieces; not a full regiment left out of the whole of it; and half the officers killed."[23] "We've been driven pell-mell through Gettysburg, and things look bad enough, I tell you."

This is the substance of the information we gain by diligent questioning of scores. It is of such stuff that the "news

[21] Maj. Gen. Winfield Scott Hancock of Pennsylvania, who commanded the Second Corps, took charge of the Union defense upon his arrival on the battlefield between 4:00 and 4:30 on the afternoon of July 1.

[22] The Eleventh Corps, commanded by Maj. Gen. Oliver Otis Howard of Maine, contained a significant number of regiments made up of men of German birth or descent. Many native-born soldiers in the Army of the Potomac disliked the "foreigners" in the Eleventh Corps and excoriated them for their performances at Chancellorsville, where they had been routed on May 2, 1863, and on the first day at Gettysburg, where they once again were driven from the field. That many of the regiments fought well at Gettysburg was lost on most observers.

[23] Maj. Gen. James Samuel Wadsworth, a member of one of the most prominent families in New York State, commanded a division in the Union First Corps. On May 6, 1864, he was mortally wounded in the battle of the Wilderness.

direct from the battlefield," made up by itinerant liars and "reporters" at points twenty or thirty miles distant, and telegraphed thence throughout the country, is manufactured. So long as the public, in its hot haste, insists on devouring the news before it is born, so long must it expect such confusion and absurdity.

Riding through the columns became more and more difficult as we advanced; and finally, to avoid it, we turned off into a by-way on the right. We were fortunately well supplied with maps, and from these we learned that but a few miles to the right of the Taneytown road, up which we had been going, ran the great Baltimore turnpike to Gettysburg; and a Dutch farmer told us that our bypath would bring us out, some miles ahead, on this pike. It was certain to be less obstructed, and we pushed on.

Across the hills to the left we could see the white-covered wagons slowly winding in and out through the forests and the masses of blue coats toiling forward. In either direction for miles you could catch occasional glimpses of the same sight through the openings of the foliage. The shades of evening dimmed and magnified the scene till one might have thought the hosts of Xerxes,[24] in all the glory of modern armor, were pressing on Gettysburg. To the front and right lay broad, well-tilled farms, dotted here and there with mammoth, many windowed barns, covered with herds and rustling with the ripening grain.

Selecting a promising looking Dutch house, with a more than usually imposing barn in its rear, we stopped for supper. The good man's "woman" had gone to see the soldiers on the road, but whatever he could get for us "you be very heartily welcome to." Great cherry trees bent before the door under their weight of ripe fruit; the kitchen garden was crowded with vegetables; contented cattle stood about the barn; sleek horses filled the stables; fat geese hissed a doubtful welcome

---

[24] The king of Persia (486–465 B.C.) who mounted an unsuccessful effort to conquer Greece in 480 B.C.

as we came too near them; the very farmyard laughed with plenty.

We put it on the ground of resting our horses and giving them time for their oats; but I fear the snowy bread and well spread table of the hearty farmer had something to do with the hour that we spent.

Then mount and spur again. It was dark in the woods, but our bypath had become a neighborhood wagon road, and the moon presently cast us occasional glances from behind the clouds. The country was profoundly quiet; the Dutch farmers seemed to have all gone to bed at dark, and only their noisy house dogs gave signs of life as we passed. Once or twice we had to rouse a sleeping worthy out of bed for directions about the road. At last campfires gleamed through the woods; presently we caught the hum of soldiers' talk ahead; by the roadside we passed a house where all the lights were out, but the family were huddled on the doorstep, listening to the soldiers. "Yes, the army's right down there. If you want to stay all night, turn up by the school-house. 'Squire Durboraw's a nice man'."

"Right down there" was the post-village of Two Taverns—thronged with soldiers—the women all in the streets, talking and questioning and frightening themselves at a terrible rate. A corps general's headquarters had been there today, but they were now moved up to the front. That didn't look like serious disaster. We were four miles and a quarter or a half from the line of battle. Ewell had come down from York, and we had been fighting him today. A. P. Hill was also up coming by way of Chambersburg or Hagerstown. Longstreet was known to be on the way and would certainly be here tomorrow.[25] The reserves were on their way. In short,

---

[25] Lt. Gen. Richard Stoddert Ewell, a native of Georgetown, District of Columbia, commanded the Confederate Second Corps. Some of his troops had reached the Susquehanna River before being recalled to concentrate with the rest of the Army of Northern Virginia near Gettysburg. Lt. Gen. Ambrose Powell Hill of Virginia led the Confederate Third Corps, elements of which opened the battle of Gettysburg on July 1; Lt. Gen.

Lee's whole army was rapidly concentrating at Gettysburg, and tomorrow, it seemed, must bring the battle that is to decide the invasion. Today it had opened for us—*not* favorably. "Squire Durboraw *is* a nice man." We roused him out of bed, where he must have been for two or three hours. "Can you take care of us and our horses till morning?" "I will do it with pleasure, gentlemen." And no more words are needed. The horses are housed in one of those great horse palaces these people build for barns; we are comfortably and even luxuriously quartered. If the situation is as we hope, our army must attack by daybreak. At any rate, we are off for the field at four in the morning.

The Repulse on Wednesday, First July

Field of Battle, near Gettysburg, July 2

To the Front

We were in the saddle this morning a little after daybreak. The army was cut down to fighting weight; it had shaken off all retainers and followers—all but its fighters; and the road was alive with this useless material.

My companion and myself were forcing our way as fast as possible through the motley crowd toward the front, where an occasional shot could already be heard, and where we momentarily expected the crash of battle to open, when I was stopped by some one calling my name from a little frame dwelling, crowded with wounded soldiers. It proved to be Colonel Luther S. Stephenson, the librarian of Congress. He had run away from his duties in the Capital, and all day yes-

---

James Longstreet, Lee's senior subordinate, commanded the Confederate First Corps.

terday, through a fight that we now know to have been one of the hottest in the war, had been serving most gallantly as aid on General Solomon Meredith's staff. Congress should make an example of its runaway official![26] The lower story of the house was crowded with wounded from the old "Iron Brigade" of Wadsworth's division; in a little upper room was their General. He had been grazed on the head with a fragment of shell, his horse had been shot under him and had fallen upon him; he had been badly bruised externally and worse internally, and there was little prospect of his being ready for service again for months. He spoke proudly of the conduct of his men, almost tearfully of their unprecedented losses.

Half a mile further on, through crowds of slightly wounded, and past farmhouses converted into hospitals, a turn to the right through a meadow, up the slope of an exposed hill, and by the side of a smouldering camp-fire. Stretched on the ground, and surrounded by his staff, lies General Wadsworth, (late Republican candidate for Governor of New York,) commander of the advance division in yesterday's fight. He, too, kindles as he tells the story of the day, its splendid fighting, and the repulse before overwhelming numbers.

Batteries are all about us; troops are moving into position; new lines seem to be forming, or old ones extending. Two or three general officers, with a retinue of staff and orderlies, come galloping by. Foremost is the spare and somewhat stooped form of the Commanding General. He is not cheered, indeed is scarcely recognized. He is an approved corps General, but he has not yet vindicated his right to command the Army of the Potomac. By his side is the calm, hon-

---

[26] Brig. Gen. Solomon Meredith, a native of North Carolina who moved to Indiana as a young man, commanded the 1st Brigade of the 1st Division of the Union First Corps. Known as the Iron Brigade and comprised of three regiments from Wisconsin and one each from Michigan and Indiana, Meredith's unit was one of the best, and perhaps the most famous, in the Army of the Potomac.

Brig. Gen. James Samuel Wadsworth

est, manly face of General Oliver O. Howard. An empty coat sleeve is pinned to his shoulder—memento of a hard fought field before, and reminder of many a battle scene his splendid Christian courage has illumined.[27] They are arranging the new line of battle. Howard's dispositions of the preceding night are adopted for the centre; his suggestions are being taken for the flanks. It is manifest already that we are no longer on the offensive, that the enemy had the initiative.

The Position

A little further forward, a turn to the left, we climb the slope of another hill, hitch our horses halfway up under cover of the woods, make our way through frowning batteries and by long rows of tombstones, stop for an instant to look at the monument of a hero from Fair Oaks, and are startled by the buzzing hiss of a well-aimed Minie from the foes that fought us at Fair Oaks, above our heads, move forward to an ambitious little gate-keeper's lodge at the entrance of the cemetery.

In front on a gradual declivity an orchard of gnarled old leafy trees; beyond the valley, a range of hills but little lower than that on which we stand; on this slope, half hidden among the clusters of trees, a large cupola-crowned brick building—a theological seminary;[28] between this and us half a dozen spires, roofs of houses, distinguishable amid the luxuriant foliage, streets marked by the lines of trees— Gettysburg!

No sound comes up from the deserted town, no ringing of bells, no voices of children, no hum of busy trade. Only now and then a blue curl of smoke rises and fades from some high window; a faint report comes up, and perhaps the hiss of a Minie is heard; the houses are not wholly without occupants.

[27] Howard had suffered a wound at the battle of Seven Pines (or Fair Oaks) on May 31, 1862, that resulted in the amputation of his right arm.

[28] The Lutheran Theological Seminary, which stood about three-quarters of a mile west of Gettysburg on Seminary Ridge.

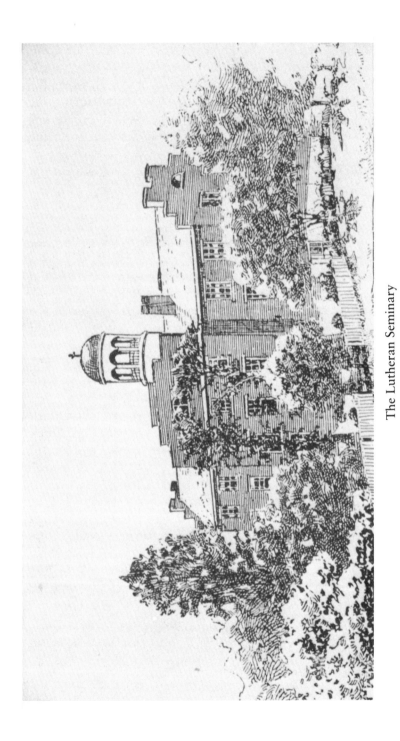

The Lutheran Seminary

We are standing on Cemetery Hill, the key to the whole position the enemy occupies, the centre of our line and the most exposed point for a concentration of the rebel fire. To our right and a little back, is the hill on which we have just left General Wadsworth; still farther back and sweeping away from the cemetery almost like the side of a horse-shoe from the toe, is a succession of other hills, some covered with timber and undergrowth, others yellow in the morning sunlight, and waving with luxuriant wheat; all crowned with batteries that are soon to reap other than a wheaten harvest. To the left, our positions are not so distinctly visible; though we can make out our line stretching off in another horse-shoe bend, behind a stone fence near the cemetery—unprotected, farther on; affording far fewer advantageous positions for batteries, and manifestly a weaker line on our right. An officer of General Howard's staff pointed out the positions to me, and I could not help hazarding the prediction that there on our left wing would come the rebel attack we were awaiting.

General Howard's headquarters were on this very Cemetery Hill—the most exposed position on the whole field. He had now returned and was good enough during the lull that still lasted, while we awaited the anticipated attack, to explain the action of yesterday as he saw it.

The Battle of Wednesday

I have now conversed with four of the most prominent generals employed in that action and with any numbers of subordinates. I am a poor hand to describe battles I do not see, but in this case I must endeavor to weave their statements into a connected narrative. The ground of the action is still in the enemy's hands, and I have no knowledge of it save from the description of others, and the distant view one gets from Cemetery Hill.

We had been advancing toward York. It was discovered

that the rebels were moving for a concentration farther south, and we suddenly changed our own line of march. The First corps, Major General John F. Reynolds, had the advance; next came the unfortunate Eleventh corps, with a new record to make that should wipe out Chancellorsville, and ready to do it.

Saturday they had been at Boonsboro, twelve or fifteen miles to the northwest of Frederick; by Tuesday night, the First corps lay encamped on Marsh Creek, within easy striking distance of Gettysburg. The Eleventh corps was ten or twelve miles farther back. Both were simply moving under general marching orders, and the enemy was hardly expected yet for a day or two.

At an early hour in the forenoon the First corps was filing down around Cemetery Hill in solid column, and entering the streets of Gettysburg. In the town our skirmishers had met pickets or scouts from the enemy and had driven them pell-mell back. The news fired the column, and General Reynolds with little or no reconnaissance marched impetuously forward. Unfortunate haste of a hero, gone now to the hero's reward!

It was fifteen minutes past ten o'clock. The fire of the rebel skirmishers rattled along the front, but shaking it off as they had the dew from their night's bivouac, the men pushed hotly on.

Meantime General Reynolds, on receiving his first notice an hour ago from Brigadier General John Buford's cavalry,[29] that the rebels were in the vicinity of Gettysburg, had promptly sent word back to General Howard, and asked him, as a prudential measure, to bring up the Eleventh corps as rapidly as possible. The Eleventh had been coming up on the Emmitsburg road. Finding it crowded with the train of the First, they had started off on a byway, leading into the

---

[29] Brig. Gen. John Buford, born in Kentucky and reared there and in Illinois, commanded the 1st Division of the Cavalry Corps in the Army of the Potomac, two brigades of which offered the initial resistance to Confederate infantry moving toward Gettysburg on July 1.

Maj. Gen. John Fulton Reynolds

Taneytown road, some distance ahead; and were still on this byway eleven miles from Gettysburg when Reynolds's messenger reached them. The fine fellows, with stinging memories of not wholly merited disgrace at Chancellorsville, started briskly forward, and a little after one their advance brigade was filing through the town to the music of the fire above. General Reynolds's corps consists of three divisions—Wadsworth's, Major General Abner Doubleday's, and Brigadier General John C. Robinson's. Wadsworth's (composed of Brigadier General Solomon Meredith's and Major General Lysander Cutler's brigades—both mainly Western troops) had the advance, with Cutler on the right and Meredith on the left.[30] Arriving at the Theological Seminary above the town, the near presence of the enemy became manifest, and they placed a battery in position to feel him out and gradually moved forward.

An engagement of more or less magnitude was evidently imminent. General Reynolds rode forward to select a position for a line of battle. Unfortunate—sadly unfortunate again—alike for him with all a gallant soldier's possibilities ahead of him and for the country, that so sorely needed his well-trained services. He fell almost instantly, pierced by a ball from a sharpshooter's rifle, and was borne, dying or dead, to the rear. General Doubleday was next in command.

The enemy was seen ready. There was no time to wait for orders from the new corps commander; instantly, right and left, Cutler and Meredith wheeled into line of battle on the double quick. Well tried troops, those; no fear of *their* flinching; veterans of a score of battles—in the war some of

---

[30] Wadsworth led the 1st Division of the First Corps, Brig. Gen. John Cleveland Robinson of New York the 2nd Division, and Maj. Gen. Abner Doubleday, another New Yorker, the 3rd Division. Doubleday commanded the corps after Reynolds's death, while Brig. Gen. Thomas Algeo Rowley of Pennsylvania replaced him at the head of the 3rd Division. Brig. Gen. Lysander Cutler of Massachusetts led the 2nd Brigade of Wadsworth's division, which contained four regiments from New York and one each from Indiana and Pennsylvania.

them from the very start; with the first at Philippi, Laurel Hill, Carrick's Ford, Cheat Mountain and all the Western Virginia campaign, trusted of Shields at Winchester, and of Lander at Romney and Bloomery Gap;[31] through the campaign of the Shenandoah Valley, and with the Army of the Potomac in every march to the red slaughter sowing that still had brought no harvest of victory. Meredith's old Iron Brigade was the Nineteenth Indiana, Twenty-fourth Michigan, Sixth and Seventh Wisconsin—veterans all, and well mated with the brave New Yorkers whom Wadsworth also led.

Cutler, having the advance, opened the attack; Meredith was at it a few minutes later. Short, sharp fighting, the enemy handsomely repulsed, three hundred rebel prisoners taken, Brigadier General James J. Archer[32] himself reported at their head—such was the auspicious opening. No wonder the First determined to hold its ground.

Yet they were ill prepared for the contest that was coming. Their guns had sounded the tocsin for the Eleventh, but so they had too for—Ewell, already marching down from York to rejoin Lee. They were fighting two divisions of A. P. Hill's now—numerically stronger than their dwindled three. Their batteries were not up in sufficient numbers; on Meredith's left—a point that especially needed protection, there were none at all. A battery with Buford's cavalry stood near. Wadsworth cut red tape and in an instant ordered it up. The Captain, preferring red tape to red fields, refused to obey. Wadsworth ordered him under arrest, could find no officer for the battery, and finally fought it under a sergeant. Sergeant and captain there should henceforth exchange places.

---

[31] Reid alludes to the fact that some of the soldiers in the First Corps had fought in 1862 under Brig. Gen. James Shields (a native of Ireland who settled in Illinois) in the Shenandoah Valley and under Brig. Gen. Frederick West Lander (a native of Massachusetts) in western Virginia.

[32] A Marylander who had practiced law before the war, Brig. Gen. James Jay Archer led a brigade in A. P. Hill's Third Corps. He remained in a Union prison for more than a year after his capture on July 1 and died shortly after his release.

The enemy repulsed, the First advanced their lines and took the position lately held by the rebels. Very heavy skirmishing, almost developing at times into a general musketry engagement, followed. Our men began to discover that they were opposing a larger force. Their own line, long and thin, bent and wavered occasionally, but bore bravely up. To the left, where the fire seemed the hottest, there were no supports at all, and Wadsworth's division, which had been in the longest, was suffering severely.

About one o'clock Major General Howard, riding in advance of his hastening corps, arrived on the field and assumed command. Carl Schurz[33] was thus left in command of the Eleventh while Doubleday remained temporarily Reynolds's successor in the First.

The advance of the Eleventh soon came up and was thrown into position to the right of the First. They had little fighting immediately—but their time was coming. Meantime the First, that had already lost its General commanding and had held its ground against superior numbers, without supports, from ten till nearly two, took fresh courage as another corps came up, and all felt certain of winning the day.

But alas! the old, old game was playing. The enemy was concentrating faster than we. Perhaps no one was to blame for it; no one among the living at least, and the thickly clustering honors that fitly crown the hero's grave bar all criticism and pardon all mistakes, if mistakes they were.

About half-past two that afternoon, standing where we now stand, on Cemetery Hill, one might have seen a long, gray line, creeping down the pike and near the railroad on the northeast side of the town. Little pomp in their march, but much haste; few wagons, but the ammunition trains all up; and the battle flags that float over their brigades are not our flags. It is the road from *York*—these are Stonewall Jackson's

[33] Maj. Gen. Carl Schurz, a native of Prussia and one of the most prominent German-born citizens of the United States, commanded the 3rd Division of the Eleventh Corps before replacing Howard at the head of the corps.

men[34]—led now by Stonewall Jackson's most trusted and loved Lieutenant [Ewell]. That gray serpent, bending in and out through the distant hills, decides the day.

They are in manifest communication with Hill's corps, now engaged, fully advised of their early losses, and of the exact situation. They bend up from the York road, debouch in the woods near the crest of the hill, and by three o'clock, with the old yell and the old familiar tactics, their battleline comes charging down.

Small resistance is made on our right. The Eleventh does not flee wildly from its old antagonists, as at their last meeting when Stonewall Jackson scattered them as if they had been pigmies, foolishly venturing into the war of the Titans. It even makes stout resistance for a little while; but the advantage of position, as of numbers, is all with the rebels, and the line is forced to retire. It is done deliberately and without confusion, till they reach the town. Here the evil genius of the Eleventh falls upon it again. To save the troops from the terrible enfilading fire through the streets, the officers wheel them by detachments into cross streets, and attempt to march them thus around one square after another, diagonally, through the town. The Germans are confused by the maneuvre; perhaps the old panic at the battle cry of Jackson's flying corps comes over them; at any rate they break in wild confusion, some pouring through the town [in] a rout, and are with difficulty formed again on the heights to the southward. They lose over one thousand two hundred prisoners in twenty minutes. One of their Generals, Alexander Schimmelfennig, an old officer in the Russian service in the Crimean War, is cut off, but he shrewdly takes to cover, conceals himself somewhere in the town, and finally escapes.[35]

But while our right is thus suddenly wiped out, how

[34] Lt. Gen. Thomas Jonathan "Stonewall" Jackson, a Virginian, had commanded the Confederate Second Corps until his death on May 10, 1863, in the wake of the battle of Chancellorsville.

[35] Brig. Gen. Alexander Schimmelfennig, like Carl Schurz a native of Prussia, led the 1st Brigade in Schurz's 1st Division of the Eleventh Corps.

fares it with the left—Robinson, and Doubleday, and sturdy Wadsworth, with the Western troops? Sadly enough.

By half-past three, as they counted the time, the whole of A. P. Hill's corps, acting in concert now with Ewell, precipitated itself upon their line. These men are as old and tried soldiers as there are in the war, and they describe the fire that followed as the most terrific they have ever known. In a single brigade, (Cutler's,) in twenty minutes, every staff officer had his horse shot under him, some of them two and three. In thirty minutes not a horse was left to General or staff, save one, and that one—as if the grim mockery of war there sought to outdo itself—had his tail shot off! General Cutler himself had three horses shot under him.

Few troops could stand it. All of the First corps could not. Presently the thin line of fire began to waver and bend and break under those terrible volleys from the dark woods above. The officers, brave almost always to a fault, sought to keep them in. One—his name deserves to be remembered— Captain Hollon Richardson of the Seventh Wisconsin seized the colors of a retreating Pennsylvania regiment and strove to rally the men around their flag. It was in vain; none but troops that have been tried as by fire can be reformed under such a storm of death; but the captain, left alone and almost in the rebels' hands, held on to the flaunting colors of another regiment, that made him so conspicuous a target, and brought them safely off.[36]

The right of the corps gave way. The fierce surge of Ewell's attack had beaten up to their front, and, added to Hill's heavy fire, forced them slowly back.

When Schurz assumed corps command, Schimmelfennig took over the division. Separated from his troops during their retreat into Gettysburg on the afternoon of July 1, Schimmelfennig hid in a small outbuilding (often described as a pigsty) for the remainder of the battle.

[36] In his official report of the battle, Gen. Doubleday mentioned that Richardson "rode up and down the lines, waving a regimental flag and encouraging the men to do their duty."

Wadsworth still holds on—for a few minutes more his braves protract the carnival of death. Doubleday managed to get three regiments over to their support; Colonel James Biddle's Pennsylvania regiment came in and behaved most gallantly.[37] Colonel Stephenson, who all the day had been serving in the hottest of the fight as aid to Meredith, relieved a wounded colonel, and strove to rally his regiment. Meredith himself, with his Antietam wound hardly yet ceasing to pain him, is struck again, a mere bruise, however—on the head, with a piece of shell. At the same instant his large, heavy horse falls, mortally wounded, bears the General under him to the ground, and beats him there with his head and shoulders in his death convulsions.

It is idle fighting Fate. Ewell turned the scale with the old, historic troops; brave men may now well retire before double their number equally brave. When the Eleventh corps fell back, the flank of the First was exposed; when the right of the First fell back, Wadsworth's flank was exposed; already flushed with their victory, rebels were pouring up against front and both flanks of the devoted brigades. They had twice cleared their front of rebel lines; mortal men could now do no more. And so, "slowly and sullenly firing," the last of them came back.

Meantime, the fate of the army had been settled. It was one of those great crises that come rarely more than once in a lifetime. For Major General Howard, brave, one-armed, Christian fighting hero, the crisis had come.

His command—two corps of the Grand Army of the Potomac—were repulsed, and coming back in full retreat, a few sturdy brigades in order, the most in sad confusion. One cavalry charge; twenty minutes' well-directed cannonading, might wipe out nearly a third of the army, and leave Meade powerless for the defence of the North. These corps must be saved, and saved at once.

[37] Reid may have confused James C. Biddle, an officer on Meade's staff, with Col. Chapman Biddle, whose 1st Brigade of Doubleday's division contained one New York and three Pennsylvania regiments.

General Howard met and overmastered the crisis. The Cemetery Hill was instantly selected.[38] The troops were taken to the rear and reformed under cover. Batteries hurried up, and when the rebel pursuit had advanced halfway through the town a thunderbolt leaped out from the whole length of that line of crest and smote them where they stood. The battle was ended, the corps were saved.

The last desperate attack lasted nowhere along the line over forty minutes; with most of it hardly over half so long. One single brigade, that "iron" column that held the left, went in one thousand eight hundred and twenty strong. It came out with seven hundred men. A few were prisoners; a few concealed themselves in houses and escaped—near a thousand of them were killed and wounded. Its fellow brigade went in one thousand five hundred strong; it came out with forty-nine officers and five hundred and forty-nine men killed and wounded, and six officers and five hundred and eighty-four men missing and their fate unknown. Who shall say that they did not go down into the very Valley of the Shadow of Death on that terrible afternoon?

Thursday's Doubtful Issue—Friday's Victory

Field of Battle near Gettysburg, Pa., July 4

Two more days of such fighting as no Northern State ever witnessed before, and victory at last! Victory for a fated army, and salvation for the imperilled country!

It were folly for one unaided man, leaving the ground

[38] One of the many controversies about the battle of Gettysburg concerns who selected Cemetery Hill as the principal Union defensive position. For a discussion of this question, see A. Wilson Greene, "From Chancellorsville to Cemetery Hill: O. O. Howard and Eleventh Corps Leadership," in Gary W. Gallagher, ed., *The First Day at Gettysburg: Essays on Confederate and Union Leadership* (Kent, Ohio: Kent State University Press, 1992), pp. 69–71.

Fighting on Seminary Ridge, July 1, 1863

within a few hours after the battle has died fitfully out, to undertake a minute detail of the operations on all parts of the field. I dare only attempt the merest outline of its leading features—then off for Cincinnati by the speediest routes. I have been unable even to learn all I sought concerning the part some of our own Ohio regiments bore—of individual brigades and regiments and batteries I can in the main say nothing. But what one man, not entirely unfamiliar with such scenes before, *could* see, passing over the ground before, during, and after the fight, I saw; for the rest I must trust to such credible statements by the actors as I have been able to collect.

The Battle-Field

Whoever would carry in his mind a simple map of our positions in the great battles of Thursday and Friday, the second and third, at Gettysburg, has but to conceive a broad capital A, bisected by another line drawn down from the top and equi-distant from each side. These three straight lines meeting at the top of the letter are the three roads along which our army advanced, and between and on which lay the battlefield. The junction of the lines is Gettysburg. The middle line, running nearly north and south, is the road to Taneytown. The right-hand line, running southeast, is the Baltimore pike. That on the left is the Emmitsburg road.[39]

Almost at the junction of the lines, and resting on the left-hand side of the Baltimore pike, is the key to the whole position—Cemetery Hill. This constitutes our extreme front, lies just south of Gettysburg, overlooks and completely commands the town; the entire valley to right and left, the whole

---

[39] Although Reid uses the image of a "broad capital A" to characterize the Union line, most writers describe it as approximating a great fishhook—with the point of the hook at Culp's Hill, the curve at East Cemetery Hill and Cemetery Hill, and the shank running south along Cemetery Ridge to Little Round Top and Round Top.

space over which the rebels advanced to attack our centre, and a portion of the woods from which the rebel lines on their centre debouched.

Standing on this hill and facing north (toward the town) you have, just across the Baltimore pike, another hill, almost as high, and crowned like the Cemetery with batteries that rake the centre front.[40] Farther to the right and rear, the country is broken into a series of short, billowy ridges, every summit of which affords a location for a battery. Through these passes the little valley of Rock Creek, crossing the Baltimore turnpike a couple of miles or so from town, and thus affording a good covered way for a rebel movement to attempt (by passing down the valley from the woods beyond this range of hills) to pierce our right wing, and penetrate to the rear of our centre.

On the left the hills are lower, afford fewer eligible positions for batteries, and are commanded by the heights on the rebel side.

The space between these lines is rolling, and in parts quite hilly; partially under cultivation, the rest lightly timbered; passable nearly everywhere for infantry and cavalry, in most parts for artillery also.

Our Line of Battle

The reader can now in an instant trace for himself our line of battle on the bisected A. Near the apex, the Cemetery, of course; batteries around the crest; infantry in line of battle down the declivity, in the orchard, and sweeping over the Taneytown road and up to that to Emmitsburg. Then along the stone fence which skirts the hither side of the Emmitsburg road for say half a mile. Then, bending in from the road a little, leaving its possession to our skirmishers alone, and so

[40] The high ground just across the Baltimore Pike from Cemetery Hill is East Cemetery Hill.

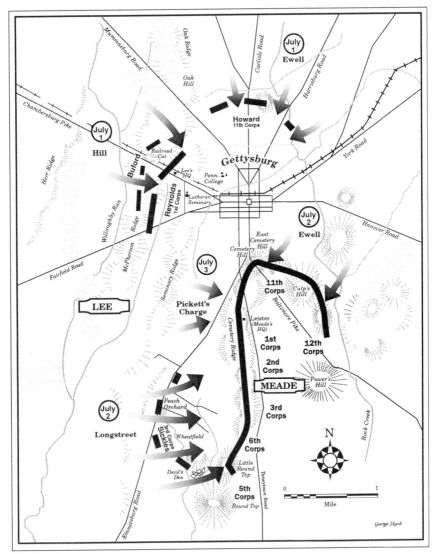

Battlefield at Gettysburg

passing back for a mile and a half farther, in a line growing more and more distant from the Emmitsburg road, and nearer that to Taneytown. These are the lines of centre and left. Beginning at the Cemetery again, our right stretches *across* the Baltimore pike and along the range of hills already described, in a direction that grows nearly parallel with the pike, (at a distance from it of a quarter to half a mile,) and down it a couple of miles. Measuring all its sinuosities, the line must be about five miles long.

The Rebel Lines and Order of Battle

All the country fronting this remarkable horseshoe line is virtually in the hands of the rebels. It will be seen that their lines must be longer than ours, and that in moving from one point to another of the field they are compelled to make long detours, while our troops can be thrown from left to right, or from either to centre, with the utmost ease and by the shortest routes.

Take the crescent of the new moon, elongate the horns a little, turn the hollow side toward our positions, and you have the general direction the rebels were compelled to give their line of battle. As was seen in Wednesday's fight, Jackson's old corps under Ewell formed their left—opposite our right; while A. P. Hill held their centre, and Longstreet, who arrived early Thursday morning, their right.

Our Order of Battle

On our front the line of battle was arranged by General Meade, at an early hour on Thursday morning, as follows: On the centre, holding Cemetery Hill and the declivity in its front, Major General Howard with his Eleventh corps. Across the pike on the adjacent hill to the right, what was left of the First corps. Next to it, and stretching to our extreme

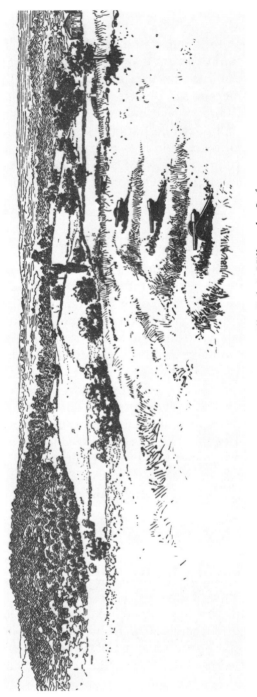

Union Batteries on Cemetery Hill, Culp's Hill to the Left

right, Major General Henry W. Slocum with his Twelfth corps. Beginning again at the Cemetery Hill, and going toward the left, we have first, next to Howard, the Second corps, Major General Hancock; next to it, the Third, Major General Daniel E. Sickles; and partly to the rear of the Third, and subsequently brought up on the extreme left, the Fifth corps, Major General George Sykes. The Sixth corps, Major General John Sedgwick, was kept near the Taneytown pike in the rear, and constituted the only reserve of the army.

Corps and Division Commanders

General readers are scarcely likely to be interested in minute details of the organization of the army, but perhaps it will be convenient to have a roster by corps and divisions, at least.[41]

First Corps—Major General John F. Reynolds.

After General Reynolds's death, General John Newton was assigned by General Meade to the command of this corps.

First Division ..... Brigadier General James S. Wadsworth.
Second Division .... Major General Abner Doubleday.
Third Division ...... Brigadier General John C. Robinson.

[41] Reid's list of corps and division commanders contains a number of errors. Doubleday first took over the First Corps after Reynolds's death; Meade later replaced Doubleday with Maj. Gen. John Newton (Doubleday remained embittered for the rest of his life about Meade's action). As note 29 indicates, Robinson commanded the 2nd and Doubleday the 3rd Division in the First Corps. In the Third Corps of Maj. Gen. Daniel Edgar Sickles, Maj. Gen. David Bell Birney led the 1st Division until called upon to replace the wounded Sickles on July 2; Brig. Gen. John Henry Hobart Ward then assumed command of the 1st Division. Brig. Gen. Romeyn Beck Ayres led the 2nd Division of Sykes's Fifth Corps. The Twelfth Corps contained just two divisions: Brig. Gen. Alpheus Starkey Williams led the 1st and Brig. Gen. John White Geary the 2nd.

Second Corps—Major General Winfield S. Hancock.

First Division .... Brigadier General John C. Caldwell.
Second Division .... Brigadier General John Gibbon.
Third Division .... Brigadier General Alexander Hays.

Third Corps—Major General Daniel E. Sickles.

First Division .... Brigadier General John H. H. Ward.
Second Division ... Brigadier General Andrew A. Humphreys.

Fifth Corps, (lately Meade's,) Major General George Sykes.

First Division .... Brigadier General James Barnes.
Second Division .... General Sykes.

Eleventh Corps—Major General Oliver O. Howard.

First Division .... Major General Carl Schurz.
Second Division ... Brigadier General Adolph von Steinwehr.
Third Division ...... Brigadier General Francis C. Barlow.

Twelfth Corps—Major General Henry W. Slocum.

First Division .... Brigadier General John W. Geary.
Second Division ...... Brigadier General George S. Greene.
Third Division .... Brigadier General Alpheus S. Williams.

Of John Sedgwick's splendid Sixth corps, which only became engaged as reserves, were brought in on Friday, I cannot give the division commanders now, (there have been such changes since Fredericksburg,) with any assurance of accuracy.[42]

Our Concentration at Gettysburg

Our troops were not concentrated so early as those of the rebels, and but for their caution in so long feeling about

[42] Maj. Gen. John Sedgwick of Connecticut commanded the Sixth Corps, in which Brig. Gen. Horatio Gouverneur Wright led the 1st Division, Brig. Gen. Albion Parris Howe the 2nd Division, and Maj. Gen. John Newton the 3rd Division. Brig. Gen. Frank Wheaton replaced Newton when Meade appointed Newton to command the First Corps.

our lines before making an attack, we might have suffered in consequence. Sedgwick's corps did not all get up till nearly dark Thursday evening, having been sent away beyond Westminster with a view to the intended movement on York. The Twelfth corps had arrived about sunset, Wednesday evening, a couple of hours or more after our repulse beyond Gettysburg; the Second and Third during that night, and the Fifth about ten Thursday morning. For Thursday's fight the Fifth constituted the only reserve.

Thursday till Four O'clock

All Thursday forenoon there was lively firing between our skirmishers and those of the enemy, but nothing betokening a general engagement. Standing on Cemetery Hill, which, but for its exposed position, constituted the best point of observation on the field, I could see the long line of our skirmishers stretching around centre and left, well advanced, lying flat on the ground in the meadows or cornfields and firing at will as they lay. The little streak of curling smoke that rose from their guns faded away in a thin vapor that marked the course of the lines down the left. With a glass the rebel line could be even more distinctly seen, every man of them with his blanket strapped over his shoulder—no foolish "stripping for the fight" with these trained soldiers. Occasionally the gray-coated fellows rose from cover, and with a yell rushed on our men, firing as they came. Once or twice in the half-hour that I watched them, they did this with such impetuosity as to force our skirmishers back, and call out a shell or two from our nearest batteries—probably the very object their officers had in view.

Toward noon I rode over to general headquarters, which had been established in a little, square, one-story, whitewashed frame house,[43] to the left and rear of the ceme-

---

[43] The Leister farmhouse on the eastern slope of Cemetery Ridge.

tery, and just under the low hill where our left joined the center. No part of the line was visible from the spot, and it had been chosen, I suppose, because while within a three minutes' gallop of the Cemetery, or the hither portion of the left, it seemed comparatively protected by its situation. The choice was a bad one. Next to the Cemetery, it proved the hottest point on the field.

General Meade had finished his arrangement of the lines. Reports of the skirmishing were coming in; the facts developed by certain reconnaissances were being presented; the trim, well tailored person of Major General Alfred Pleasonton[44] was constantly passing in and out; the cavalry seemed to be in incessant demand. General Williams and Major Simon F. Barstow, the Adjutant Generals, were hard at work sending out the orders; aids and orderlies were galloping off and back; General G. K. Warren, Acting Chief of Staff, was with the General Commanding, poring over the maps of the field which the engineers had just finished; most of the staff were stretched beneath an apple tree, resting while they could.[45]

It seemed that a heavy pressure had been brought to bear for an attack on the enemy by the heads of columns in divisions, pouring the whole army on the enemy's centre, and smashing through it after the old Napoleonic plan; but Meade steadily resisted. The enemy was to fight him where he stood, was to come under the range of this long chain of batteries on the crests. Wisely decided, as the event proved.

[44] Maj. Gen. Alfred Pleasonton, born in Washington, D.C., commanded the Cavalry Corps in the Army of the Potomac. His extensive postwar writings about Gettysburg and other aspects of the war are highly unreliable.

[45] An admiring fellow staff officer remarked that Maj. Simon Forrester Barstow discharged his duties "with the offhand way of an old workman." On June 28, 1863, Maj. Gen. Gouverneur Kemble Warren of New York, the chief engineer in the army, had turned down Meade's invitation to become chief of staff. Reid erred in calling him the acting chief of staff; Maj. Gen. Daniel Butterfield, also a native of New York, had been Hooker's chief of staff and retained his position under Meade.

Meade's Headquarters

The afternoon passed on in calm and cloudless splendor. From headquarters I rode down the left, then back to Slocum's headquarters on a high hill,[46] half or three quarters of a mile south from the Cemetery, on the Baltimore pike. Everywhere quiet, the men stretched lazily on the ground in line of battle, horses attached to the caissons, batteries unlimbered and gunners resting on their guns.

The thunderbolts were shut up, like Aeolus's winds;[47] it seemed as if the sun might set in peace over all this mighty enginery of destruction held in calm, magnificent reserve.

The Rebel Attack on the Left

But unseen hands were letting loose the elements. General Meade had not failed to see the comparatively exposed position of our left; and between three and four the order was sent out for the extreme left—then formed by Sickles's (Third) corps—to advance. If the enemy was preparing to attack us there, our advance would soon unmask his movements.[48]

It did. The corps moved out, spiritedly, of course—when even in disastrous days did it go otherwise to battle?—and by four o'clock had found the rebel advance.[49] Longstreet was bringing up his whole corps—nearly a third of the rebel army—to precipitate upon our extreme left. The fight at once opened with artillery first, presently with crashing

[46] Slocum's headquarters was on Power's Hill.

[47] In Greek mythology, Aeolus was the god of the winds.

[48] On July 2, Sickles decided to advance without Meade's approval, an action that triggered a longstanding controversy. Sickles would argue that his movement saved the Army of the Potomac; others insisted that it nearly cost the North a victory. For two opposing views, see Richard A. Sauers, *A Caspian Sea of Ink: The Meade–Sickles Controversy* (Baltimore: Butternut and Blue, 1989), and William Glenn Robertson, "The Peach Orchard Revisited: Daniel E. Sickles and the Third Corps on July 2, 1863," in Gary W. Gallagher, ed., *The Second Day at Gettysburg: Essays on Confederate and Union Leadership* (Kent, Ohio: Kent State University Press, 1993).

[49] The next several paragraphs describe action at the Peach Orchard salient, in the Wheatfield, and at Devil's Den and Little Round Top.

roars of musketry, too. Rebel batteries were already in position, and some of them enfiladed Sickles's line. Our own were hastily set to work, and the most dangerous of the rebel guns were partially silenced. Then came a rebel charge with the wild yell and rush; it is met by a storm of grape and canister from our guns depressed to rake them in easy range. The line is shattered and sent whirling back on the instant. Long columns almost immediately afterward begin to debouch from the woods to the rear of the rebel batteries—another and a grander charge is preparing. General Warren who, as Chief of Staff, is overlooking the fight for the Commanding General, sends back for more troops. Alas! Sedgwick's corps is not yet available. We have only the Fifth for the reserves. Howard and Hancock are already at work on the centre and left centre. But Hancock advances, and the fire grows intenser still along the whole line of the left.

Meantime, Cemetery Hill is raked at once from front and left, and the shells from rebel batteries on the left carry over even into the positions held by our right. The battle rages on but one side, but death moves visibly over the whole field from line to line and front to rear. Trains are hurried away on the Baltimore pike; the unemployed *debris* of the army takes alarm, a panic in the rear seems impending. Guards thrown hastily across the roads to send the runaways back, do something to repress it.

The rebel lines we have seen debouching behind their batteries on Sickles's front slowly advance. The fight grows desperate, aid after aid is sent for reinforcements; our front wavers, the line of flame and smoke sways to and fro, but slowly settles backward. Sickles is being—not driven—but pushed back. At last the reserve comes in; the advance of the brigades of the Fifth wind down among the rocks and enter the smoke, the line braces up, advances, halts soon, but comes no more back. The left is not overpowered yet. We had had two hours of exceedingly severe artillery and musketry fighting. The enemy still holds a little of the ground we had, but the chances seem almost even.

One Phase—A Type of Many

I cannot trace the movements further in detail; let me give one phase of the fight, fit type of many more. Some Massachusetts batteries—Captain John Bigelow's, Captain Charles A. Phillips's, two or three more under Captain Freeman McGilvery of Maine[50]—were planted on the extreme left, advanced now well down to the Emmitsburg road, with infantry in their front—the first division, I think, of Sickles's corps. A little after five a fierce rebel charge drove back the infantry and menaced the batteries. Orders are sent to Bigelow on the extreme left, to hold his position at every hazard short of sheer annihilation, till a couple more batteries can be brought to his support. Reserving his fire a little, then with depressed guns opening with double charges of grape and canister, he smites and shatters, but cannot break the advancing line.[51] His grape and canister are exhausted, and still, closing grandly up over their slain, on they come. He falls back on spherical case, and pours this in at the shortest range. On, still onward comes the artillery-defying line, and still he holds his position. They are within six paces of the guns—he fires again. Once more, and he blows devoted soldiers from his very muzzles. And still mindful of that solemn

---

[50] Capt. John Bigelow's 9th Battery of Massachusetts Light Artillery and Capt. Charles A. Phillips's 5th Battery (E) of Massachusetts Artillery were part of Lt. Col. Freeman McGilvery's 1st Volunteer Brigade of Artillery. These cannon supported Sickles's infantry near the Peach Orchard.

[51] Here and below, Reid mentions different types of artillery ammunition. Grape shot was a round made up of 9 to 21 large balls attached to a core of wood or metal; a round of canister consisted of a tin cylinder filled with 27 to 48 cast iron shot. Especially deadly at a range of 300 to 600 yards, both types of rounds when fired broke apart into a pattern similar to that of a shotgun. Spherical case (or Shrapnel) was a hollow cast-iron container filled with lead musket balls and designed to explode above ground, sending missiles down into the target. With an effective range of 500 to 1,500 yards, spherical case probably would have been fired before grape or canister. Gun carriages, made of wood and iron, supported the tube or barrel of a cannon; caissons were two-wheeled, horse-drawn vehicles that carried artillery ammunition.

order, he holds his place. They spring upon his carriages and shoot down his horses! And then, his Yankee artillerists still about him, he seizes the guns by hand, and from the very front of that line drags two of them off. The caissons are further back—five out of the six are saved.

That single company, in that half-hour's fight, lost thirty-three of its men, including every sergeant it had. The Captain himself was wounded. Yet it was the first time it was ever under fire! I give it simply as a type. *So* they fought along that fiery line!

The rebels now poured on Phillips's battery, and it, too, was forced to drag off the pieces by hand when the horses were shot down. From a new position it opened again; and at last the two reinforcing batteries came up on the gallop. An enfilading fire swept the rebel line; Sickles's gallant infantry charged, the rebel line swept back on a refluent tide—we regained the lost ground, and every gun just lost in this splendid fight.

Once more I repeat, this is but a type.

Reinforcements Called in from the Right

Slocum, too, came into the fight. The reserves were all used up; the right seemed safe. It was believed from the terrific attack that the whole rebel army, Ewell's corps included, was massed on our centre and left; and so a single brigade was left to hold the rifle-pits constructed through the day along the whole line of the Twelfth on the right; and the rest of the corps came across the little neck of land to strengthen our weakening line. Needful, perhaps, but perilous in the extreme.[52]

[52] Slocum dispatched Williams's division and two brigades of Geary's division to assist hard-pressed Union defenders in the area of the Wheatfield; only the brigade of Brig. Gen. George Sears Greene, a 62-year-old Rhode Islander who was among the oldest field commanders in Federal service, remained on Culp's Hill to resist the assaults of Ewell's corps during the evening of July 2.

The Close

At six the cannonade grew fiercer than ever, and the storm of death swept over the field from then till darkness ended the conflict. In the main our strengthened columns held the line. At points they were forced back a little; a few prisoners were lost. On the whole the rebels were unsuccessful, but we had not quite held our own.

Some caissons had been blown up on either side; a barn on the Emmitsburg road was fired by the rebel shells, and its light gave their sharpshooters a little longer time at that point to work. Both sides lay on their arms exhausted, but insatiate, to wait for the dawning.

Results and Doubtful Issue

The Third and Second corps were badly shattered. The Eleventh had not been quite so much engaged—its artillery had kept the rebels at a greater distance—but it had behaved well. Sickles was wounded—a leg shot off; General Samuel K. Zook was killed; our own old townsman Colonel Edward E. Cross was killed; the farm houses and barns for miles were filled with the wounded. The rebels had left us William Barksdale, dying; what other losses they had met we could only conjecture from the piles of dead the last rays of the sun had shown along their front.[53]

And so, with doubtful prospects, darkness came like a wall between us, and compelled nature's truce.

[53] Brig. Gen. Samuel Kosciuszko Zook, a Pennsylvanian, fell leading his 3rd Brigade of Caldwell's division of the Second Corps in fighting at the Wheatfield; Col. Edward E. Cross, a native of New Hampshire whose colorful prewar career included duels fought in Arizona and Mexico, commanded the 1st Brigade in Caldwell's division and also received his mortal wound in the Wheatfield. On the Confederate side, Brig. Gen. William Barksdale, a native of Tennessee long associated with Mississippi and a brigade commander in Longstreet's First Corps, was mortally wounded in the vicinity of the Trostle farm.

From the right there came sudden, sharp volleys of cheers; Ewell had *not* gone; a hasty rush had carried some of Slocum's rifle-pits, protected only by the long drawn out line of a single brigade. It was a gloomy close. That was our strongest point, where Jackson's men had gained their fortified foothold.[54]

Now, indeed, if ever, may the nation well wrestle with God in prayer. We have fought but three hours and a half; have lost on both flanks; have called every reserve we had on the field into action, and with daybreak must hold these shattered columns to the work again. Well may the land take up the refrain of George Henry Boker's touching hymn for the Philadelphia Fourth.

> "Help us, Lord, our only trust!
> We are helpless, we are dust!
> All our homes are red with blood;
> Long our grief we have withstood;
> Every lintel, each door post,
> Drips, at tidings from the host,
> With the blood of some one lost.
> Help us, Lord, our only trust!
> We are helpless, we are dust!"

The Opening—Friday Morning

I must be pardoned some egotism in what remains. It is easiest to narrate what one has seen, and undue prominence may thus come to be given to certain points, for time and space press me more and more.

At day break crashing volleys woke the few sleepers there were. A fusilade ran along the line—each had felt the other, then came cautious skirmishing again.

---

[54] Reid must have considered Culp's Hill, held by Greene's brigade of Slocum's corps, as the strongest Union point because its elevation exceeded that of Cemetery Hill. He referred to Ewell's soldiers as Stonewall Jackson's men because the Confederate Second Corps originally had been Jackson's.

But on the right there was no cessation. Ewell's men were in possession of part of our riflepits, and sought to gain the remainder; Slocum must defend the one part and regain the other at every hazard. They were fighting Stonewall Jackson's men—it might well be desperate work. I had gone down the Baltimore pike at night to find a resting-place—coming up between four and five, I heard clearly on the right the old charging cheer. Once, twice, three times I counted it, as my horse pushed his way for less than a mile through the curious or coward throng that ebbed and flowed along the pike. Each time a charge was made, each time the musketry fire leaped out from our line more terrific than before, and still the ground was held. To the left and centre, firing gradually ceased. All interest was concentrated on this fierce contest on the right; the rest of the line on either side was bracing itself for still more desperate work.

From four to five there was heavy cannonading also, from our batteries nearest the contested points, but the artillery fire diminished and presently ceased. The rebels made no reply; we were firing at random, and it was a useless waste of ammunition. A cloud of smoke curled up from the dark woods on the right; the musketry crash continued with unparalleled tenacity and vehemence, wounded men came back over the fields, a few stragglers were hurried out to the front, ammunition was kept conveniently near the line.

In the fields to the left of the Baltimore pike stood the reserve artillery, with horses harnessed to the pieces and ready to move on the instant. Cavalry, too, was drawn up in detachments here and there. Moved over already within supporting distance of Slocum's line stood a part of Sedgwick's corps, (the reserve of today,) ready for the emergency that seemed likely soon to demand it. Occasional bullets from the rebel front spattered against the trees and fences. Now and then a Minie[55] went over with its buzzing hiss, but the pike

[55] The most common infantry projectile of the Civil War was called the minié ball—a hollow base, lead bullet of cylindro-conoidal shape produced in .58 and other calibers. A pair of French army captains named

was too nearly out of range to be cleared of the watching throng.

General Sickles

Through this throng with slow tread there came a file of soldiers, armed, but marching to the rear. It was a guard of honor for one who well deserved it. On a stretcher, borne by a couple of stout privates, lay General Sickles—but yesterday leading his corps with all the enthusiasm and dash for which he has been distinguished—today with his right leg amputated, and lying there, grim and stoical, with his cap pulled over his eyes, his hands calmly folded across his breast, and *a cigar in his mouth!* For a man who had just lost a leg, and whose life was yet in imminent jeopardy, it was cool indeed. He was being taken to the nearest railroad line, to be carried to some city where he could get most careful attendance; and the guard that accompanied him showed that already there was some apprehensions for the rear.

There was reason for it. Less than an hour later orders were issued from Pleasonton's headquarters, a mile or so further back on the Baltimore pike, for Colonel J. Irvin Gregg[56] to take his cavalry force and guard against a dash down the valley of Rock Creek into the rear and centre. The rebels met the preparation and drew back to try it soon again further out the line.

The Battle on the Right[57]

I rode up the high hill where General Slocum's headquarters were established; but though it afforded an excellent

---

Henri-Gustave Delvigne and Claude-Étienne Minié developed the bullet in the 1840s.

[56] Col. John Irvin Gregg led the 3rd Brigade of Brig. Gen. David McMurtrie Gregg's 2nd Division of the Union Cavalry Corps. Both Pennsylvanians, the Gregg's also were distantly related.

[57] Reid terms the climax of the struggle for Culp's Hill on the morning of July 3 "The Battle on the Right."

Maj. Gen. Daniel Edgar Sickles

view of most of our positions, the fight going on was concealed by a mask of woods on the distant hills. The Rodman guns[58] on the hill were all manned, and the gunners were eager to try their range, but it still seemed useless. Firing in the woods, they were as likely to hit friend as foe. Signal officers here were in communication with general headquarters, with Howard on Cemetery Hill, Hancock next [to] him on the right, and one or two of the headquarters on the left. There was no fear of lack of certain communication between the different portions of the field, let the fortunes of the day go what way they would.

As I rode down the slope and up through the wheat fields to Cemetery Hill, the batteries began to open again on points along our outer line. They were evidently playing on what had been Slocum's line of yesterday. The rebels, then, were there still, in our rifle pits. Presently the battery on Slocum's hill gained the long-sought permission, and opened, too, aiming apparently in the same direction. Other batteries along the inner line, just to the left of the Baltimore pike, followed the signal, and as one after another opened up, till every little crest between Slocum's headquarters and Cemetery Hill began belching its thunder, I had to change my course through the wheat fields to avoid our own shells.

Still no artillery response from the rebels. Could they be short of ammunition? Could they have failed to bring up all their guns? Were they, perhaps, massing artillery elsewhere, and only keeping up this furious crash of musketry on the right as a blind?

By eight o'clock I had reached Cemetery Hill. Yesterday's conflict was more plainly inscribed on the tombstones than the virtues of the buried dead they commemorated. Shells had ploughed up lately sodded graves; round shot had shattered marble columns; dead horses lay about among the monuments, and the gore of dead men soaked the soil and moistened the roots of flowers on the old graves.

[58] Rodman 3-inch rifles were cast iron cannon with a maximum range of approximately 2,800 yards.

This morning it was comparatively quiet again. Sharp-shooters from the houses in the town were picking off officers who exposed themselves along the crest. They knew that we did not want to shell the place, and presumed upon the fore-bearance of our artillery. The annoyance had at last become too serious, and one of our guns had been directed to dis-lodge a nest of the most audacious and the surest aimed by battering down the house from which they were firing. It was the only house in Gettysburg we harmed throughout the battles.

To the front skirmishers were still at work, but in a des-ultory way. All eyes were turned to the right; where now that our artillery had taken its share in the contest, its intensity seemed but redoubled by Ewell's men. Distinctly, even amid all this roar, there came up the sound of another of those ominous cheers; and the hurricane of crashing sound that fol-lowed seemed tearing the forest trees and solid hillside asun-der. It was another rebel charge. Standing by the gatekeeper's lodge, with a glass I could distinctly see our shattered line swinging irregularly and convulsively back from those death-bearing woods. The rebel yells redoubled, but so did our artillery fire, now that the gunners saw exactly where to throw. The retreat lasted for but a moment, the line straight-ened, rallied, plunged into the woods again.

A Tried General

All this while—the fire gradually getting a little hotter on the hill, and an occasional shell from the rebel guns, now beginning to open, coming over—General Howard was calmly reclining against a hillock by a grave stone, with his staff about him. One or two he kept constantly watching the right, and occasionally sweeping the whole rebel line with their glasses; the rest were around him, ready for instant ser-vice. I have seen many men in action, but never so imperturb-ably cool as this General of the Eleventh corps. I watched him closely as a Minie whizzed overhead. *I* dodged, of course; I never expect to get over that habit; but I am confident he did not move a muscle by the fraction of a hair's breadth.

Progress on the Right

About a quarter after nine the conflict in the woods to the right seemed to be culminating. Clouds of smoke obscured the view, but beyond that smoke we knew that our noble line—the Twelfth and a part of the First with some reserves were now engaged—was holding its ground; the direction of the sound even seemed to indicate that it was gaining, but of course that was a very uncertain test. "Ride over to General Meade," said Howard to one of his aids, "and tell him the fighting on the right seems more terrific than ever and appears swinging somewhat toward the centre, but that we know little or nothing of how the battle goes, and ask him if he has any orders." In a few minutes the aid galloped back. "The troops are to stand to arms, sir, and watch the front."

Meantime there was a little diversion away down toward the extreme right. A brigade had been thrown east of Rock Creek to watch the possible attempt at repeating the effort to get down the valley into our rear. Finding a good opportunity, it began to pour in its volleys upon Ewell's flank. The audacity of a single brigade attempting such a thing was beyond rebel suspicion; they naturally thought a heavy force was turning their flank, and were less inclined to push on Slocum's sorely pressed men in front.

Nothing seemed to come of Howard's "watching the front"; the fire of skirmishers revived occasionally and then died away again; and finally, about a quarter before ten, I started over to general headquarters. In descending the Cemetery Hill and crossing the intervening fields, I noticed that some bullets were beginning to come over from our left, but supposed them of course to be merely stray shots from the rebel skirmishers.

Maj. Gen. Oliver Otis Howard

The Commander-in-Chief at Headquarters

Headquarters presented a busy scene. Meade was receiving reports in the little house, coming occasionally to the door to address a hasty inquiry to some one in the group of staff officers under the tree. Quick and nervous in his movements, but calm, and as it seemed to me, lit up with the glow of the occasion, he looked more the General, less the student. Polished, fashionable looking Pleasonton, riding whip resting in the leg of one of his jackboots, and neatly fitting kids drawn over his hands, occasionally put in some earnest remark. Warren, calm, absorbed, earnest as ever, was constantly in consultation with the Commander.

In all matters of detail, Williams or Major Barstow was referred to as to an encyclopedia. Orderlies and aids were momentarily dashing up with reports and off with orders; the signal officers were bringing in the reports telegraphed by the signal flags from the different crests that overlooked the fight. The rest of the staff stood ready for any duty, and outside the little garden fence a great group of horses stood hitched.

Headquarters Under Fire

Wilkeson, my original companion from Baltimore, was up at last and very sad. His son, a gallant young lieutenant of regular artillery, had had his leg shot off in Wednesday's disastrous fight, and whether living now or dead he could not tell; he was a prisoner (or a corpse) in Gettysburg.[59]

We walked around to the east of the little house and lay down on the grass. Others were there; there was much comparison of views, talk of probabilities, gossip of the arrival of militia from Harrisburg. The fight still raged furiously on the right. Headquarters were under a slight fire. The balls from

[59] Lt. Bayard Wilkeson, commanding Battery G, Fourth U.S. Artillery in Howard's Eleventh Corps, was mortally wounded almost immediately after entering the battle north of Gettysburg on July 1.

Lt. Bayard Wilkeson and His Artillery Battery, July 1, 1863

the left seemed to increase a little in number; a few came over from the front; we saw no damage that any of them did.

Close by our heads went one, evidently from some kind of small arm that had an unfamiliar sound. "That," said Wilkeson, aesthetic always or nothing, "that is a muffled howl; that's the exact phrase to describe it." We discussed the question.

Wh-r-sh-shh! A sudden exclamation and start all around the group. "Jove!" exclaims one, impulsively; "those fellows on the left have the range of headquarters exactly." It was a round shot that had passed not two feet from the door and buried itself in the road three or four yards in front of us. In an instant there was another and another. General Meade came to the door, told the staff that they manifestly had our range, and that they had best go up the slope fifteen or twenty yards to the stable. As they started, a couple of shells came, then more from a different direction, and a sharp fusillade broke out just behind us on the left. Two rebel batteries clearly had our range, and the fight seemed opening up on the field of last night's bitterest contest.

A few minutes before, I had been talking of going down to look at Barksdale's corpse—there was other work to do than looking at dead men now. Leaving the late headquarters to the shells, I galloped out the Taneytown road along the left. For three quarters of a mile the fire was bursting out.[60]

The air was alive with all mysterious sounds, and death in every one of them. There were "muffled howls" that seemed in rage because their missile missed you, the angry buzz of the familiar Minie, the *spit* of the common musket ball, hisses, and the great whirring rushes of shells. And then there came others that made the air instinct with warning, or quickened it with vivid alarm; long wails that fatefully

[60] The artillery fire Reid describes here was that of Confederate batteries directed against Cemetery Ridge preparatory to Pickett's and Pettigrew's assault on the afternoon of July 3. It compelled Meade, his staff, and orderlies to abandon the Leister house and killed at least sixteen of their horses.

bemoaned the death they wrought; fluttering screams that filled the whole space with their horror, and encompassed one about as a garment; cries that ran the diapason of terror and despair.

Rise and Ebb of the Tide of Battle

It had been a sudden concentration of terrific artillery fire on our left, with a view to silence our batteries and sweep resistance from the slopes before they charged. But they did not find us unprepared. The tornado of death that swept over the fields levelled much before it, but not all. After an hour or two it was found that the obstinate defenders still clung to their positions; and the rebels saw they must reserve their energies for the more determined and persistent effort the afternoon was to bring. On it, as on the last toss of the dice, they had staked their all. In an hour or two the left was silent again; on the centre there was but the accustomed straggling shots.[61]

The Right Victorious

Meantime on the right, the fierceness of Ewell's attack had dashed itself out, and but feeble surges came up now against our line. Leaving the left as the attack there was dying away, I rode over again to Slocum's Hill on the Baltimore pike. From this high eminence we could only make out that the line seemed in its old place, and so the officers said it was. The rifle pits had been regained; Ewell's corps had been substantially repulsed. The musketry still flickered sharply up

[61] For an excellent account of the Confederate bombardment by the officer who directed it, see Edward Porter Alexander, *Fighting for the Confederacy: The Personal Recollections of General Edward Porter Alexander,* ed. Gary W. Gallagher (Chapel Hill, N.C.: University of North Carolina Press, 1989), pp. 247–62.

occasionally, but the fire had gone out of it. We were practically victorious on the right. It was a quarter past eleven—seven hours and a quarter of desperate fighting! The old Jackson corps had not given up without an obstinate struggle.

Cavalry—A Lull

Away down from the extreme right, and apparently beyond it, there came a ripple of musketry. It was said to be William F. Smith's division from Major General Darius N. Couch's Harrisburg force, coming in on Ewell's flank or rear. I have not yet been able to satisfy myself whether the report was true or not.[62]

A quarter of an hour later Pleasonton's scouts reported rebel cavalry coming in on the Bonaughtown road on the right to strike the Baltimore pike in our rear. Gregg was instantly sent off to meet them, with orders merely to hold them in check, and not to bring on a close engagement if he could avoid it. At the same time Brigadier General Judson Kilpatrick was ordered to the extreme left to harass the enemy's flank and rear and look after his trains. "Good!" exclaimed Kilpatrick, rubbing his hands, and in a moment was hurrying gleefully to execute the order.[63]

Gregg threw his force up a little brook that comes down between Rock Creek and the post village of Two Taverns.

---

[62] Maj. Gen. Darius Nash Couch of New York commanded the Department of the Susqehanna, in which thousands of militia, emergency troops, and other second-line units provided indifferent support to the Army of the Potomac. Brig. Gen. William Farrar Smith, a Vermonter known as "Baldy" in the Union army, led several thousand of the untried troops in Couch's department. On July 8, Smith described his force as an "incoherent mass" with which he could accomplish nothing. The report that Couch and Smith were coming in on Ewell's flank or rear was not true.

[63] Brig. Gen. Hugh Judson Kilpatrick of New Jersey led the 3rd Division of the Union Cavalry Corps. On the afternoon of July 3, troopers under his command launched a futile attack against Confederate infantry on the southern end of the battlefield.

The rebel cavalry no sooner saw their plan detected than they retired. But their effort was not over, and fortunately Gregg understood it. Under cover of the woods, they moved still further south, in a direction parallel with the Baltimore pike; but Gregg was moving too, and when they started out toward the pike, they were again confronted. There was a little carbine firing now, and some sharp shelling, and the rebels again retired. Once more they came out, almost opposite Two Taverns, late in the afternoon, but Gregg was still on the watch for them, and they at once and finally retired without a shot.

There was a lull from a quarter past eleven to about one. Fitful firing broke out and died away again here and there, but the lines were mainly silent. The rebels were not yet defeated—except for the hour's sharp work on the left, two of their corps with their reserves had not been engaged at all today. Some final desperate effort must be maturing. Shrewd officers predicted that it would be a massing of all their troops on the left. But Ewell's corps could not possibly be brought over in time for that; its work for the day must be nearly done.

The Last Desperate Attack

Pretty soon the attack came[64]—sooner, indeed, and wider than was expected. About one the rebel movement was developed in a thunder of cannonading that rolled over our army like doom. They had concentrated immense quantities of artillery—"two hundred and fifty pieces, at least,"[65] some of General Meade's staff-officers said, on our centre and left, and those devoted lines were to bear the last, fiercest shock, that, staunchly met, should leave the exhausted rebel army drifting back from its supreme effort, a defeated host. Long-

---

[64] Reid here refers to Pickett's and Pettigrew's assault, which marked the grand climax of the battle of Gettysburg.

[65] This estimate is too large by approximately one hundred guns.

street and A. P. Hill were to support and follow up the artillery attack, and the reserves were with them.

Soon, from the Cemetery hill, (I did not see this, but tell it as actors in it told me,) could be seen the forming columns of Hill's corps. Their batteries had already opened in almost a semicircle of fire on that scarred hill front. Three cross fires thus came in upon it, and today the tracks of shells ploughing the ground in as many directions may be seen everywhere among the graves. Howard never moved his headquarters an inch. There was his Eleventh corps, and there he meant to stay and make them do their duty if he could. They did it well.

When the fierce cannonade had, as they supposed, sufficiently prepared the way, down came the rebel lines, "dressed to the right" as if for a parade before some grand master of reviews. To the front they had a line of skirmishers, double or treble the usual strength, next the line of battle for the charge, next another equally strong in reserve, if the fierce fire they might meet should melt away the first.

Howard sent orders for his men to lie down, and for a little our batteries ceased firing. The rebels thought they had silenced us and charged. They were well up to our front when that whole corps of concealed Germans sprang up and poured out their sheet of flame and smoke, and swiftly flying death; the batteries opened—the solid lines broke, and crisped up into little fragments, and were beaten widely back. Our men charged; company after company, once at least a whole regiment, threw down their arms and rushed over to be taken prisoners and carried out of this fearful fire.

Simultaneously, similar scenes were enacting along the front of the Second, Third, and Fifth corps. Everywhere the rebel attack was beaten back, and the cannonade on both sides continued at its highest pitch.

When this broke out, I had been coming over from the neighborhood of Pleasonton's headquarters. Ascending the high hill to the rear of Slocum's headquarters, I saw such a sight as few men ever hope to see twice in a lifetime. Around our centre and left, the rebel line must have been from four to five miles long, and over that whole length there rolled up the smoke from their two hundred and fifty guns. The roar, the bursting bombs, the impression of magnificent power, "all the glory visible, all the horror of the fearful field concealed," a nation's existence trembling as the clangor of those iron monsters swayed the balance—it was a sensation for a century!

About two the fire slackened a little, then broke out deadlier than ever, till, beaten out against our impenetrable sides, it ebbed away, and closed in broken, spasmodic dashes.

The great, desperate, final charge came at four.[66] The rebels seemed to have gathered up all their strength and desperation for one fierce, convulsive effort, that should sweep over and wash out our obstinate resistance. They swept up as before, the flower of their army to the front, victory staked upon the issue. In some places they literally lifted up and pushed back our lines, but, that terrible "position" of ours!—wherever they entered it, enfilading fires from half a score of crests swept away their columns like merest chaff. Broken and hurled back, they easily fell into our hands, and on the centre and left the last half-hour brought more prisoners than all the rest.

So it was along the whole line; but it was on the Second corps that the flower of the rebel army was concentrated; it was there that the heaviest shock beat upon and shook and even sometimes crumbled our line.

We had some shallow rifle pits, with barricades of rails from the fences. The rebel line, stretching away miles to the left, in magnificent array, but strongest here—Pickett's[67] splendid division of Longstreet's corps in front, the best of A. P. Hill's veterans in support—came steadily and as it seemed

---

[66] Reid places the time of the assault at least an hour too late.

[67] Maj. Gen. George Edward Pickett, a native of Virginia, commanded a division in Longstreet's corps that made up less than half of the Confederate attack column but nonetheless has come to be synonymous with the famous assault.

resistlessly sweeping up. Our skirmishers retired slowly from the Emmitsburg road, holding their ground tenaciously to the last. The rebels reserved their fire till they reached this same Emmitsburg road, then opened with a terrific crash. From a hundred iron throats, meantime, their artillery had been thundering on our barricades.

Hancock was wounded; Gibbon succeeded to the command—a proved soldier and ready for the crisis.[68] As the tempest of fire approached its height, he walked along the line and renewed his orders to the men to reserve their fire. The rebels—three lines deep—came steadily up. They were in point blank range.

At last the order came! From thrice six thousand guns there came a sheet of smoky flame, a crash, a rush of leaden death. The line literally melted away; but there came a second, resistless still. It had been our supreme effort—on the instant we were not equal to another.

Up to the rifle pits, across them, over the barricades— the momentum of their charge, the mere machine strength of their combined action swept them on. Our thin line could fight, but it had not weight enough to oppose to this momentum. It was pushed behind the guns. Right on came the rebels. They were upon the guns, were bayoneting the gunners, were waving their flags above our pieces.

But they had penetrated to the fatal point. A storm of grape and canister tore its way from man to man and marked its track with corpses straight down their line! They had exposed themselves to the enfilading fire of the guns on the western slope of Cemetery Hill; that exposure sealed their fate.[69]

[68] Brig. Gen. John Gibbon, a native of Philadelphia reared in North Carolina, led the 2nd Division of the Second Corps.

[69] Enfilading fire hits a defensive line from the side or end rather than from the front. It is especially effective because shots that miss the initial target may strike soldiers farther down the line; defenders, moreover, cannot return the fire effectively because they run the risk of hitting their own comrades.

Maj. Gen. Winfield Scott Hancock

The line reeled back—disjointed already—in an instant in fragments. Our men were just behind the guns. They leaped forward upon the disordered mass; but there was little need for fighting now. A regiment threw down its arms, and with colors at its head rushed over and surrendered. All along the field small detachments did the same. Webb's brigade[70] brought in eight hundred taken in as little time as it requires to write the simple sentence that tells it. Gibbon's old division took fifteen stand of colors.

Over the fields the escaped fragments of the charging line fell back—the battle there was over. A single brigade, Brigadier General William Harrow's, (of which the Seventh Michigan is part,) came out with fifty-four less officers, seven hundred and ninety-three less men than it took in![71] So the whole corps fought—so too they fought further down the line.

Finis

It was fruitless sacrifice. They gathered up their broken fragments, formed their lines, and slowly marched away. It was not a rout, it *was* a bitter crushing defeat. For once the Army of the Potomac had won a clean, honest, acknowledged victory.

Yet we were very near defeat. Our ammunition had grown scant; the reserve ammunition train had been brought up and drained; but for that we should have been left to cold steel.

Brigade after brigade had been thrown forward to strengthen the line; as the rebel attack drifted back over the fields there stood in the rear just one single brigade that con-

[70] Brig. Gen. Alexander Stewart Webb was a New Yorker whose brigade was the 2nd of Gibbon's division.

[71] A native of Kentucky reared in Illinois, Brig. Gen. William Harrow led the 1st Brigade of Gibbon's division and took over the division when Gibbon replaced the wounded Hancock in corps command.

stituted the entire reserve of the Army of the Potomac. Forty thousand fresh troops to have hurled forward upon that retreating mass would have ended the campaign with the battle; but, for forty thousand we had that one wasted brigade! The rebels were soon formed again, and ready for defence— the opportunity was lost!

Shells still dropped over the Cemetery, by the headquarters and in the wheat fields toward the Baltimore pike; but the fight was over.

Headquarters were established anew under the trees in a little wood near Slocum's Hill. General Meade rode up, calm as ever, and called for paper and aids; he had orders already to issue. A band came marching in over the hillside; on the evening air its notes floated out—significant melody—"Hail to the Chief."

"Ah! General Meade," said W., "you're in very great danger of being President of the United States." "No," said another, more wisely, as it seems. "Finish well this work so well begun, and the position you have is better and prouder than President."

After the Battle

Our campaign "after the invaders" was over. There was brief time for last glances at the field, last questions after the dead and dying—then the hurried trip west, and the misery of putting together, from the copious notes taken on the field, on swaying railroad cars, and amid jostly crowds, the story of the day.

The morning after the battle was as sweet and fresh as though no storm of death had all the day before been sweeping over those quiet Pennsylvania hills and valleys. The roads were lined with ambulances, returning to the field for the last of the wounded; soldiers exchanging greetings after the battle with their comrades and comparing notes of the day; officers looking after their wounded men or hunting up the supplies for their regiments. Detachments of rebel prisoners every few moments passed back under guard; the woods inside our line had been full of them all night, and we were just beginning to gather them up.[72] Everybody was in the most exuberant spirits. For once this army had won a real victory—the soldiers felt it, and the sensation was so novel, they could not but be ecstatic.

The Field

Along the lines on the left a sharp popping of skirmishers was still kept up. I rode down over the scene of yesterday's fiercest conflict, and at the cost of some exposure, and the close passage of a couple of Minie balls, got a view of the thickly strewn rebel corpses that still cast up to heaven their mute protest against the treason that had made them what they were. But the details of these horrible scenes are too sickening, and alas! too familiar; I must be excused from their description.

At Headquarters

Headquarters—still over in the woods near Slocum's Hill—were in bivouac. The General had a little wall tent, in which he was dictating orders and receiving despatches; General Ingalls, the Chief Quartermaster,[73] had his writing table in the open of a covered wagon; the rest, majors, colonels, generals and all, had slept on the ground, and were now standing about the campfires, hands full of fried pork and hard bread, making their breakfasts in a style that a year ago

---

[72] Casualties for the three days were enormous. The Confederates lost between 23,000 and 28,000 men, of whom more than 5,000 were prisoners; the Union army counted more than 3,000 dead, more than 14,500 wounded, and nearly 5,500 missing or captured.

[73] Brig. Gen. Rufus Ingalls of Maine. The quartermaster was responsible for the clothing, food, and other equipment exclusive of ammunition and arms needed by the army.

Confederate Prisoners on the Baltimore Pike

would have astonished the humblest private in the Army of the Potomac.

The cavalry generals were again in request, and heavy reconnaissances were ordered. The bulk of the rebel army was believed to be in full retreat; one strong corps could still be seen, strongly posted on well chosen heights to the north-ward and drawn up in line of battle to repel any attempt at direct pursuit.

The casualties on the staff were wonderfully small. General Warren, acting Chief of Staff, had a remarkable escape. A Minie ball passed directly under his chin, cut his throat in a little line that, with half an inch's motion in his head, or change in the direction of the ball, would have been converted into a deathly wound. As it was, his shirt was stained with the blood that trickled down, but he did not think the wound worth binding up.

It has been telegraphed and re-telegraphed and tele-graphed again from headquarters, that General Butterfield was badly wounded. He received a slight blow on the back Friday afternoon from a spent fragment of shell, I believe; but it did not even break the skin.

These, with the wounding of Lieutenant Colonel Joseph Dickinson, Aid to General Meade, constituted the only casu-alties on the staff.[74]

Major Barstow, the efficient Adjutant-General, received fragments of shells on both sides of his saddle but escaped unhurt.

The Fire at Headquarters

It was not, however, because they had little exposure that their losses were small. How we were nearly all driven

[74] Lt. Col. Joseph Dickinson had served on Joseph Hooker's staff, and, like Daniel Butterfield, may not have been a favorite of the new army commander. Neither Meade nor any other Federal officer mentioned the wounded Dickinson in his official report.

away from headquarters Friday forenoon by the furious cannonade has already been told; but my friend and companion
on that morning, Mr. Samuel Wilkeson of the New York
Times, has so vividly described the scene that I must be
allowed to reproduce it:

"In the shadow cast by the tiny farm house, sixteen by
twenty, which General Meade had made his headquarters,
lay wearied staff officers and tired correspondents. There was
not wanting to the peacefulness of the scene the singing of a
bird, which had a nest in a peach tree within the tiny yard of
the white washed cottage. In the midst of its warbling, a shell
screamed over the house, instantly followed by another and
another, and in a moment the air was full of the most complete artillery prelude to an infantry battle that was ever
exhibited. Every size and form of shell known to British and
to American gunnery, shrieked, whirled, moaned, and whis-
tled and wrathfully fluttered over our ground. As many as six
in a second, constantly two in a second, bursting and screaming over and around the headquarters, made a very hell of
fire that amazed the oldest officers. They burst in the yard—
burst next to the fence on both sides, garnished as usual
with the hitched horses of aides and orderlies. The fastened
animals reared and plunged with terror. Then one fell, then
another—sixteen lay dead and mangled before the fire
ceased, still fastened by their halters, which gave the expression of being wickedly tied up to die painfully. These brute
victims of a cruel war touched all hearts. Through the midst
of the storm of screaming and exploding shells, an ambulance
driven by its frenzied conductor at full speed, presented to all
of us the marvelous spectacle of a horse going rapidly on
three legs. A hinder one had been shot off at the hock. A shell
tore up the little step at the headquarters cottage, and ripped
bags of oats as with a knife. Another soon carried off one of
its two pillars. Soon a spherical case burst opposite the open
door—another ripped through the low garret. The remaining
pillar went almost immediately to the howl of a fixed shot

that Whitworth[75] must have made. During this fire the horses at twenty and thirty feet distant were receiving their death, and soldiers in Federal blue were torn to pieces in the road, and died with the peculiar yells that blend the extorted cry of pain with horror and despair. Not an orderly—not an ambulance—not a straggler was to be seen upon the plain swept by this tempest of orchestral death, thirty minutes after it commenced. Were not one hundred and twenty pieces of artillery trying to cut from the field every battery we had in position to resist their purposed infantry attack, and to sweep away the slight defences behind which our infantry were waiting? Forty minutes—fifty minutes—counted watches that ran, oh! so languidly! Shells through the two lower rooms. A shell into the chimney, that daringly did not explode. Shells in the yard. The air thicker and fuller and more deafening with the howling and whirring of these infernal missiles. The Chief of Staff struck—Seth Williams—loved and respected through the army, separated from instant death by two inches of space vertically measured. An aide bored with a fragment of iron through the bone of the arm. And the time measured on the sluggish watches was one hour and forty minutes."

How the Correspondents Faced Death

To this vivid description, in justice to its author, let me add that Mr. Wilkeson stayed at the house during the whole terrible cannonade. Mr. Frank Henry, also of the *Times,* likewise stood it out. Their accounts may well be said to have the smell of fire upon them![76]

[75] The Whitworth Rifle was a British-made cannon with a range of more than 5,000 yards. A breechloading weapon, its ammunition was loaded not from the muzzle but from the back. In a war dominated by muzzle-loading cannon with much shorter ranges, the Whitworth stood out as an exotic weapon. The Confederate army had two Whitworths at Gettysburg; the Federal artillery none.

[76] Frank Henry also stayed at the Leister house through the bombardment.

C. C. Coffin, of the Boston *Journal,* and L. L. Crounse, of the New York *Times* as well as several other journalists of whom I knew less, were at different times under almost equally heavy fire. Mr. Crounse had his horse shot under him during Thursday's engagement. Such perils are they compelled to face who would be able to say something more of a battle than what those who are first out of it, can tell.

Once More on Cemetery Hill—Departure

We could linger no longer on the field. My companion for the last day or two, Mr. Coffin, and myself, resolved on reaching Baltimore that night. The Northern Central Railroad was still broken, and from Baltimore my shortest road west lay *via* Philadelphia. With such a circuitous route ahead, there was no time to spare.

We rode up the Cemetery Hill for a last look at the field. It was ploughed and torn in every direction by the fierce crossfires of artillery that had spent their force upon it. Dead men, decently laid out, were in the gate keeper's lodge. Upturned, swollen horses lay among the tombs, where the sudden shot or shell had stricken them down. Batteries still frowned from the crest; away to the front of the rebel line (a strong rearguard only now) could still be distinctly seen. Howard, Carl Schurz, Steinwehr,[77] and two or three others of lesser rank, were watching the movements through their glasses and discussing the probabilities.

There was a rush of letters to be mailed and telegraph messages to be sent. Among the number came Henry Ward Beecher's son, a bluff hearty looking youth. He had a despatch to Mrs. Stowe he wanted me to send, announcing that

---

[77] Brig. Gen. Adolph Wilhelm August Friedrich, Baron von Steinwehr, was a native of the Duchy of Brunswick who commanded the 2nd Division of the Eleventh Corps.

The Gatekeeper's House on Cemetery Hill After the Battle

her son, too, was among the wounded and would soon be sent home to her.[78]

On an old grave that a shell had rudely torn, while a round shot had battered down the iron railing about it, were still blooming the flowers affection's hand had planted in more peaceful times—not a petal shaken off by all this tempest that had swept and whirled and torn about them. Human blood watered the roots—patriot blood that made them doubly sacred. I stooped and gathered them—roses and columbine and modest, sweet-scented pinks, mingled with sprigs of cypress—they are my only trophy from that glorious field.

Good-by to Gettysburg—a mad gallop to Westminster, (which brought our day's ride up to nearly fifty miles,) to catch a train that after all, loaded with wounded soldiers as it was, spent the whole night backing and hauling on side tracks and switches; and so at last to Baltimore; and out of the field once more. May it be forever.

EFFECT OF LEE'S ESCAPE

1863, July 17

"This puts us back into next year." Such was Vice President Hamlin's[79] exclamation as the escape of Lee's army was announced to him. That was in the midst of our forces and under all the influences that always exist there favorable to delay and apologetic for disaster. Here the feeling seems to have been at once more decided and more bitter. The Presi-

[78] Henry Ward Beecher of Connecticut, a prominent Congregationalist minister and antislavery speaker, was the brother of novelist Harriet Beecher Stowe, whose *Uncle Tom's Cabin* had deepened northern antipathy toward slavery in the 1850s. Brig. Gen. von Steinwehr's official report of the battle mentioned Mrs. Stowe's son: "Capt. F. W. Stowe, assistant adjutant general of this division, was on the last day severely wounded in the head by a piece of shell."

[79] Hannibal Hamlin of Maine was vice president during Lincoln's first term.

dent declares Lee's escape the greatest blunder of the war. Others are not wanting to cry already for some man who can pursue and fight.[80]

Justice to a man who needs all he can get of it requires me to add that, in persistency of urging action at least, General Halleck was not this time to blame. Whether he was equally energetic in furnishing and directing aright the means of action is another question. General Meade telegraphed him that there was a difference in his Council of War, and that he was hesitating about making an attack. Halleck replied: "It is proverbial that Councils of War never fight, attack the enemy at once, and hold Councils of War afterward." The order was good; but, by the time it arrived, the enemy had escaped by a pontoon bridge, which Halleck had not prevented from being sent up the south side of the Potomac.

Today it is rumored that Meade has asked to be relieved of command. It is certain that the old swarm of personal imbroglios in the Army of the Potomac has broken out again. Meantime we have crossed the river, but the indications do not foreshadow a very vigorous pursuit.[81]

[80] Meade's failure to follow up his victory at Gettysburg with a rapid pursuit of Lee's retreating army caused controversy at the time and continues to generate debate among historians. In a letter dated July 14, 1863, but never sent to the general, Lincoln congratulated Meade for "the magnificent success" at Gettysburg, yet expressed deep regret that Lee had escaped greater punishment: "I do not believe you appreciate the magnitude of the misfortune involved in Lee's escape," wrote Lincoln. "He was within your easy grasp, and to have closed upon him would, in connection with our other late successes, have ended the war. As it is, the war will be prolonged indefinitely." For an able discussion of this topic, see chapter 20 of Coddington, *The Gettysburg Campaign*.

[81] The Army of the Potomac was the most intensely political of the major Union field armies. For much of the first two years of the war, its high command had been plagued by factions maneuvering for advantage, often with the help of politicians in nearby Washington. George Meade shunned such activity. Although after Gettysburg he received much criticism, on January 28, 1864, Congress thanked him for the "skill and heroic valor which, at Gettysburg, repelled, defeated and drove back, broken and dispirited, beyond the Rappahannock, the veteran army of the rebellion."

Arthur James Lyon Fremantle

II

THE GETTYSBURG CAMPAIGN

From the Diary of A. J. L. Fremantle

20th June (Saturday).—Armed with letters of introduction from the Secretary at War for Generals Lee and Longstreet, I left Richmond at 6 A.M., to join the Virginian army. I was accompanied by a sergeant of the Signal Corps, sent by my kind friend Major Norris,[1] for the purpose of assisting me in getting on. We took the train as far as Culpeper, and arrived there at 5:30 P.M., after having changed cars at Gordonsville, near which place I observed an enormous pile of excellent rifles rotting in the open air. These had been captured at Chancellorsville; but the Confederates have already such a super-abundant stock of rifles that apparently they can afford to let them spoil. The weather was quite cool after the rain of last night. The country through which we passed had been in the enemy's hands last year, and was evacuated by them after the battles before Richmond; but at that time it was not their custom to burn, destroy, and devastate—every thing looked green and beautiful, and did not in the least give one the idea of a hot country.

In his late daring raid, the Federal General Stoneman crossed this railroad, and destroyed a small portion of it, burned a few buildings, and penetrated to within three miles of Richmond; but he and his men were in such a hurry that they had not time to do much serious harm.[2]

[1] Maj. William Norris, who subsequently received promotion to the rank of colonel, was chief of the Confederate Signal Corps.

[2] Between April 29 and May 8, 1863, Maj. Gen. George Stoneman of New York, commander of the Cavalry Corps of the Army of the Potomac during the Chancellorsville campaign, led a raid against Richmond.

Culpeper was, until five days ago, the headquarters of Generals Lee and Longstreet; but since Ewell's recapture of Winchester, the whole army had advanced with rapidity, and it was my object to catch it up as quickly as possible. On arriving at Culpeper, my sergeant handed me over to another myrmidon of Major Norris, with orders from that officer to supply me with a horse, and take me himself to join Mr. Lawley,[3] who had passed through for the same purpose as myself three days before.

Sergeant Norris, my new chaperon, is cousin to Major Norris, and is a capital fellow. Before the war he was a gentleman of good means in Maryland, and was accustomed to a life of luxury; he now lives the life of a private soldier with perfect contentment, and is utterly indifferent to civilization and comfort. Although he was unwell when I arrived, and it was pouring with rain, he proposed that we should start at once—6 P.M. I agreed, and we did so. Our horses had both sore backs, were both unfed, except on grass, and mine was deficient of a shoe. They nevertheless travelled well, and we reached a hamlet called Woodville, fifteen miles distant, at 9:30. We had great difficulty in procuring shelter; but at length we overcame the inhospitality of a native, who gave us a feed of corn for our horses, and a blanket on the floor for ourselves.

21st June (Sunday).—We got the horse shod with some delay, and after refreshing the animals with corn and ourselves with bacon, we effected a start at 8:15 A.M. We experienced considerable difficulty in carrying my small saddlebags and knapsack, on account of the state of our horses' backs. Mine was not very bad, but that of Norris was in a horrid state. We had not travelled more than a few miles when the latter animal cast a shoe, which took us an hour to

[3] Francis E. Lawley reported on the war in America for the *Times* of London. For a narrative of his time in the South, see William Stanley Hoole, *Lawley Covers the Confederacy* (Tuscaloosa, Ala.: Confederate Publishing Company, 1964).

replace at a village called Sperryville. The country is really magnificent, but as it has supported two large armies for two years, it is now completely cleaned out. It is almost uncultivated, and no animals are grazing where there used to be hundreds. All fences have been destroyed, and numberless farms burnt, the chimneys alone left standing. It is difficult to depict and impossible to exaggerate the sufferings which this part of Virginia has undergone. But the ravages of war have not been able to destroy the beauties of nature—the verdure is charming, the trees magnificent, the country undulating, and the Blue Ridge mountains form the background.

Being Sunday, we met about thirty negroes going to church, wonderfully smartly dressed, some (both male and female) riding on horseback, and others in wagons; but Mr. Norris informs me that two years ago we should have numbered them by hundreds.[4] We soon began to catch up the sick and broken-down men of the army, but not in great numbers; most of them were well shod, though I saw two without shoes.

After crossing a gap in the Blue Ridge range, we reached Front Royal at 5 P.M., and we were now in the well-known Shenandoah Valley—the scene of Jackson's celebrated campaigns.[5] Front Royal is a pretty little place, and was the theatre of one of the earliest fights in the war, which was commenced by a Maryland regiment of Confederates, who, as Mr. Norris observed, "jumped on to" a Federal regiment from the same State, and "whipped it badly." Since that time the village has changed hands continually, and was visited by the Federals only a few days previous to Ewell's rapid advance ten days ago.

After immense trouble we procured a feed of corn for

---

[4] It is an interesting question why there would be fewer black churchgoers during the war. This could indicate that many slaves from the region had seized opportunities offered by the conflict to leave their owners and seek freedom.

[5] Fremantle refers to Stonewall Jackson's successful 1862 Shenandoah Valley Campaign.

the horses, and, to Mr. Norris's astonishment, I was impudent enough to get food for ourselves by appealing to the kind feelings of two good-looking female citizens of Front Royal, who, during our supper, entertained us by stories of the manner they annoyed the Northern soldiers by disagreeable allusions to "Stonewall" Jackson.

We started again at 6:30, and crossed two branches of the Shenandoah river, a broad and rapid stream. Both the railway and carriage bridges having been destroyed, we had to ford it; and as the water was deep, we were only just able to accomplish the passage. The soldiers, of whom there were a number with us, took off their trousers, and held their rifles and ammunition above their heads. Soon afterwards our horses became very leg-weary; for although the weather had been cool, the roads were muddy and hard upon them. At 8:30 we came up with Pender's division[6] encamped on the sides of hills, illuminated with innumerable camp-fires, which looked very picturesque. After passing through about two miles of bivouacs, we begged for shelter in the hayloft of a Mr. Mason: we turned our horses into a field, and found our hayloft most luxurious after forty-six miles' ride at a foot's pace.

Stonewall Jackson is considered a regular demigod in this country.

22d June (Monday).—We started without food or corn at 6:30 A.M., and soon became entangled with Pender's division on its line of march, which delayed us a good deal. My poor brute of a horse also took this opportunity of throwing two more shoes, which we found it impossible to replace, all the blacksmiths' shops having been pressed by the troops.

The soldiers of this division are a remarkably fine body of men, and look quite seasoned and ready for any work.

---

[6] Maj. Gen. William Dorsey Pender of North Carolina commanded a division in A. P. Hill's Third Corps.

Their clothing is serviceable, so also are their boots; but there is the usual utter absence of uniformity as to color and shape of their garments and hats: gray of all shades, and brown clothing, with felt hats, predominate. The Confederate troops are now entirely armed with excellent rifles, mostly Enfields.[7] When they first turned out they were in the habit of wearing numerous revolvers and bowie-knives. General Lee is said to have mildly remarked: "Gentlemen, I think you will find an Enfield rifle, a bayonet, and sixty rounds of ammunition, as much as you can conveniently carry in the way of arms." They laughed, and thought they knew better; but the six-shooters and bowie-knives gradually disappeared; and now none are to be seen among the infantry.

The artillery horses are in poor condition, and only get 3 lb. of corn* a-day. The artillery is of all kinds—Parrotts, Napoleons, rifled and smooth bores, all shapes and sizes; most of them bear the letters U.S., showing that they have changed masters.[8]

The colors of the regiments differ from the blue battle-flags I saw with Bragg's army. They are generally red, with a blue St. Andrew's Cross showing the stars. This pattern is said to have been invented by General Joseph Johnston, as not so liable to be mistaken for the Yankee flag. The new Confederate flag has evidently been adopted from this battle-flag, as it is called. Most of the colors in this division bear the

*Indian corn.

[7] Enfield rifle muskets were produced in England and used widely in the Union and the Confederate armies.

[8] Fremantle mentions two of the most common types of field artillery found in Civil War armies: the Parrott gun, an iron rifled cannon with a reinforced breech developed by Robert Parker Parrott; and the Napoleon or Model 1857 gun, a smoothbore cannon named after French emperor Louis Napoleon, who contributed to its development. Especially effective firing canister against assaulting troops, the Napoleons were probably the most popular artillery pieces in the Union and the Confederate armies and, along with similar guns, accounted for approximately 40 percent of the cannon at Gettysburg (most of the cannon were rifled pieces of various types).

names Manassas, Fredericksburg, Seven Pines, Harper's Ferry, Chancellorsville, &c.[9]

I saw no stragglers during the time I was with Pender's division; but although the Virginian army certainly does get over a deal of ground, yet they move at a slow dragging pace, and are evidently not good marchers naturally. As Mr. Norris observed to me, "Before this war we were a lazy set of devils; our niggers worked for us, and none of us ever dreamt of walking, though we all rode a great deal."

We reached Berryville (eleven miles) at 9 A.M. The headquarters of General Lee were a few hundred yards beyond this place. Just before getting there, I saw a general officer of handsome appearance, who must, I knew from description, be the Commander-in-chief; but as he was evidently engaged I did not join him, although I gave my letter of introduction to one of his Staff. Shortly afterwards, I presented myself to Mr. Lawley, with whom I became immediately great friends.* He introduced me to General Chilton, the Adjutant-general of the army, to Colonel Cole, the Quartermaster-general, to Major Taylor, Captain Venable, and other officers of General Lee's Staff;[10] and he suggested, as the headquarters were so busy and crowded, that he and I should ride to Winchester at once, and afterwards ask for hospitality from the less busy Staff of General Longstreet. I was also introduced to Captain Scheibert, of the Prussian army, who is a guest sometimes of General Lee and sometimes of General Stuart of the cavalry.[11] He had been present at one of the late

---

*The Honorable F. Lawley, author of the admirable letters from the Southern States, which appeared in the "Times" newspaper.

[9] Gen. P. G. T. Beauregard rather than Gen. Joseph E. Johnston took the lead in designing the Confederate battle flag following the battle of First Manassas or Bull Run in July 1861.

[10] The members of Lee's staff whom Fremantle mentions were Col. Robert H. Chilton, Lt. Col. Robert G. Cole, Maj. Walter H. Taylor, and Maj. Charles S. Venable, all Virginians.

[11] Capt. Justus Scheibert spent several months in the Confederacy during 1863 and in 1868 published an account of the trip in his native German. It first appeared in English as *Seven Months in the Rebel States Dur-*

severe cavalry skirmishes, which have been of constant occur-
rence since the sudden advance of this army. This advance
has been so admirably timed as to allow of the capture of
Winchester, with its Yankee garrison and stores, and at the
same time of the seizure of the gaps of the Blue Ridge range.
All the officers were speaking with regret of the severe wound
received in this skirmish by Major Von Borcke, another Prussian, but now in the Confederate States service, and aid-de-
camp to Jeb Stuart.[12]

After eating some breakfast, Lawley and I rode ten miles
into Winchester. My horse, minus his fore-shoes, showed
signs of great fatigue, but we struggled into Winchester at 5
P.M., where I was fortunate enough to procure shoes for the
horse, and, by Lawley's introduction, admirable quarters for
both of us at the house of the hospitable Mrs. ——, with
whom he had lodged seven months before, and who was
charmed to see him. Her two nieces, who are as agreeable as
they are good-looking, gave us a miserable picture of the
three captivities they have experienced under the Federal
commanders, Banks, Shields, and Milroy.[13]

The unfortunate town of Winchester seems to have been
made a regular shuttlecock of by the contending armies.
Stonewall Jackson rescued it once, and last Sunday week his
successor, General Ewell, drove out Milroy. The name of
Milroy is always associated with that of Butler, and his rule
in Winchester seems to have been somewhat similar to that of

---

ing the North American War, 1863, translated by Joseph C. Hayes and
edited by William Stanley Hoole (Tuscaloosa, Ala.: Confederate Publishing
Company, 1958).

[12] Maj. Heros von Borcke, who was wounded in cavalry fighting
near Middleburg, Virginia, wrote of his Confederate experiences in *Memoirs of the Confederate War for Independence,* published first in *Blackwood's Edinburgh Magazine* in 1865 and subsequently reprinted several
times.

[13] Union troops under Maj. Gen. Nathaniel Prentiss Banks and Brig.
Gen. James Shields occupied Winchester at different times in 1862; Maj.
Gen. Robert Huston Milroy commanded a Federal force stationed at Win-
chester in the spring and early summer of 1863.

his illustrious rival in New Orleans. Should either of these
two individuals fall alive into the hands of the Confederates,
I imagine that Jeff Davis himself would be unable to save
their lives, even if he were disposed to do so.[14]
Before leaving Richmond, I heard every one expressing
regret that Milroy should have escaped, as the recapture of
Winchester seemed to be incomplete without him.[15] More
than 4,000 of his men were taken in the two forts which over-
look the town, and which were carried by assault by a Louisianian brigade with trifling loss. The joy of the unfortunate
inhabitants may easily be conceived at this sudden and unexpected relief from their last captivity, which had lasted six
months. During the whole of this time they could not legally
buy an article of provisions without taking the oath of alle-
giance, which they magnanimously refused to do. They were
unable to hear a word of their male relations or friends, who
were all in the Southern army; they were shut up in their
houses after 8 P.M., and sometimes deprived of light; part of
our kind entertainer's house was forcibly occupied by a vulgar, ignorant, and low-born Federal officer, *ci-devant* driver
of a street car; and they were constantly subjected to the most
humiliating insults, on pretence of searching the house for
arms, documents, &c. To my surprise, however, these ladies
spoke of the enemy with less violence and rancor than almost
any other ladies I had met with during my travels through the
whole Southern Confederacy. When I told them so, they
replied that they who had seen many men shot down in the
streets before their own eyes knew what they were talking

---

[14] Fremantle alludes here to bitter Confederate attitudes toward
Union Maj. Gen. Benjamin Franklin Butler, who presided over a controversial occupation of New Orleans in 1862. Confederate President Jefferson
Davis certainly would have made no effort to help Butler, whom he said
was "properly surnamed the Beast."

[15] At the battle of Second Winchester on June 14–15, 1863, Milroy
suffered a stinging defeat. The Federal army lost nearly 4,500 men killed,
wounded, and captured from a force of just less than 7,000, as well as 23
cannon and hundreds of wagons.

about, which other and more excited Southern women did not.

Ewell's division is in front and across the Potomac; and before I left headquarters this morning, I saw Longstreet's corps beginning to follow in the same direction.

23d June (Tuesday).—Lawley and I went to inspect the site of Mr. Mason's[16] (the Southern Commissioner in London) once pretty house—a melancholy scene. It had been charmingly situated near the outskirts of the town, and by all accounts must have been a delightful little place. When Lawley saw it seven months ago, it was then only a ruin; but since that time Northern vengeance (as directed by General Milroy) has satiated itself by destroying almost the very foundations of the house of this arch-traitor, as they call him. Literally not one stone remains standing upon another; and the *débris* seems to have been carted away, for there is now a big hole where the principal part of the house stood. Troops have evidently been encamped upon the ground, which was strewed with fragments of Yankee clothing, accoutrements, &c.

I understand that Winchester used to be a most agreeable little town, and its society extremely pleasant. Many of its houses are now destroyed or converted into hospitals; the rest look miserable and dilapidated. Its female inhabitants (for the able-bodied males are all absent in the army) are familiar with the bloody realities of war. As many as 5,000 wounded have been accommodated here at one time. All the ladies are accustomed to the bursting of shells and the sight of fighting, and all are turned into hospital nurses or cooks.

From the utter impossibility of procuring corn, I was forced to take the horses out grazing a mile beyond the town for four hours in the morning and two in the afternoon. As one mustn't lose sight of them for a moment, this occupied me all day, while Lawley wrote in the house. In the evening

---

[16] James Murray Mason, a Confederate diplomat and politician.

Francis Lawley in Later Life

we went to visit two wounded officers in Mrs. ——'s house, a major and a captain in the Louisianian brigade which stormed the forts last Sunday week. I am afraid the captain will die. Both are shot through the body, but are cheery. They served under Stonewall Jackson until his death, and they venerate his name, though they both agree that he has got an efficient successor in Ewell, his former companion in arms; and they confirmed a great deal of what General Johnston had told me as to Jackson having been so much indebted to Ewell for several of his victories. They gave us an animated account of the spirits and feeling of the army. At no period of the war, they say, have the men been so well equipped, so well clothed, so eager for a fight, or so confident of success— a very different state of affairs from that which characterized the Maryland invasion of last year, when half of the army were barefooted stragglers, and many of the remainder unwilling and reluctant to cross the Potomac.

Miss —— told me to-day that dancing and horse-racing are forbidden by the Episcopal Church in this part of Virginia.

24th June (Wednesday).—Lawley being in weak health, we determined to spend another day with our kind friends in Winchester. I took the horses out again for six hours to graze, and made acquaintance with two Irishmen, who gave me some cut grass and salt for the horses. One of these men had served and had been wounded in the Southern army. I remarked to him that he must have killed lots of his own countrymen; to which he replied, "Oh yes, but faix they must all take it as it comes." I have always observed that Southern Irishmen make excellent "Rebs," and have no sort of scruple in killing as many of their Northern brethren as they possibly can.

I saw to-day many new Yankee graves, which the deaths among the captives are constantly increasing. Wooden head-posts are put at each grave, on which is written, "An

Unknown Soldier, U.S.A. Died of wounds received upon the field of battle, June 21, 22, or 23, 1863." A sentry stopped me to-day as I was going out of town, and when I showed him my pass from General Chilton, he replied with great firmness, but with perfect courtesy, "I'm extremely sorry, sir; but if you were the Secretary of War, or Jeff Davis himself, you couldn't pass without a passport from the Provost-marshal."

25th June (Thursday).—We took leave of Mrs. —— and her hospitable family, and started at 10 A.M. to overtake Generals Lee and Longstreet, who were supposed to be crossing the Potomac at Williamsport. Before we had got more than a few miles on our way, we began to meet horses and oxen, the first fruits of Ewell's advance into Pennsylvania. The weather was cool and showery, and all went swimmingly for the first fourteen miles, when we caught up McLaws's[17] division, which belongs to Longstreet's corps. As my horse about this time began to show signs of fatigue, and as Lawley's pickaxed most alarmingly, we turned them into some clover to graze, whilst we watched two brigades pass along the road. They were commanded, I think, by Semmes and Barksdale,* and were composed of Georgians, Mississippians, and South Carolinians.[18] They marched very well, and there was no attempt at straggling; quite a different state of things from Johnston's men in Mississippi. All were well shod and efficiently clothed. In rear of each regiment were from twenty to thirty negro slaves, and a certain number of unarmed men carrying stretchers and wearing in their hats the red badges of the ambulance corps;—this is an excellent institution, for it prevents unwounded men falling out on

---

*Barksdale was killed, and Semmes mortally wounded, at the battle of Gettysburg.

[17] Maj. Gen. Lafayette McLaws of Georgia.

[18] Brig. Gen. Paul Jones Semmes of Georgia commanded a brigade of four regiments from that state; Barksdale's brigade contained four regiments of Mississippians.

pretence of taking wounded to the rear. The knapsacks of the men still bear the names of the Massachusetts, Vermont, New Jersey, or other regiments to which they originally belonged. There were about twenty wagons to each brigade, most of which were marked U.S., and each of these brigades was about 2,800 strong. There are four brigades in McLaws's division. All the men seem in the highest spirits, and were cheering and yelling most vociferously.

We reached Martinsburg (twenty-two miles) at 6 P.M., by which time my horse nearly broke down, and I was forced to get off and walk. Martinsburg and this part of Virginia are supposed to be more Unionist than Southern; however, many of the women went through the form of cheering McLaws's division as it passed. I dare say they would perform the same ceremony in honor of the Yankees to-morrow.

Three miles beyond Martinsburg we were forced by the state of our horses to insist upon receiving the unwilling hospitality of a very surly native, who was evidently Unionist in his proclivities. We were obliged to turn our horses into a field to graze during the night. This was most dangerous, for the Confederate soldier, in spite of his many virtues, is, as a rule, the most incorrigible horse-stealer in the world.

26th June (Friday).—I got up a little before daylight, and, notwithstanding the drenching rain, I secured our horses, which, to my intense relief, were present. But my horse showed a back rapidly getting worse, and both looked "mean" to a degree. Lawley being ill, he declined starting in the rain, and our host became more and more surly when we stated our intention of remaining with him. However, the sight of *real gold* instead of Confederate paper, or even greenbacks, soothed him wonderfully, and he furnished us with some breakfast. All this time McLaws's division was passing the door; but so strict was the discipline, that the only man who loafed in was immediately pounced upon and carried away captive. At 2 P.M., the weather having become a little clearer, we made a start, but under very unpromising circum-

Maj. Gen. Lafayette McLaws

stances. Lawley was so ill that he could hardly ride; his horse was most unsafe, and had cast a shoe;—my animal was in such a miserable state that I had not the inhumanity to ride him;—but, by the assistance of his tail, I managed to struggle through the deep mud and wet.

We soon became entangled with McLaws's division, and reached the Potomac, a distance of nine miles and a half, at 5 P.M.; the river is both wide and deep, and in fording it (for which purpose I was obliged to mount) we couldn't keep our legs out of the water. The little town of Williamsport is on the opposite bank of the river, and we were now in Maryland. We had the mortification to learn that Generals Lee and Longstreet had quitted Williamsport this morning at 11 o'clock, and were therefore obliged to toil on to Hagerstown, six miles further. This latter place is evidently by no means rebel in its sentiments, for all the houses were shut up, and many apparently abandoned. The few natives that were about stared at the troops with sulky indifference.

After passing through Hagerstown, we could obtain no certain information of the whereabouts of the two generals, nor could we get any willing hospitality from any one; but at 9 P.M., our horses being quite exhausted, we forced ourselves into the house of a Dutchman, who became a little more civil at the sight of gold, although the assurance that we were English travellers, and not rebels, had produced no effect. I had walked to-day, in mud and rain, seventeen miles and I dared not take off my solitary pair of boots, because I knew I should never get them on again.

27th June (Saturday).—Lawley was so ill this morning that he couldn't possibly ride. I therefore mounted his horse a little before daybreak, and started in search of the generals. After riding eight miles, I came up with General Longstreet, at 6:30 A.M., and was only just in time, as he was on the point of moving. Both he and his Staff were most kind, when I introduced myself and stated my difficulties. He arranged that an ambulance should fetch Lawley, and he immediately invited me to join his mess during the campaign. He told me (which I did not know) that we were now in Pennsylvania, the enemy's country—Maryland being only ten miles broad at this point. He declared that bushwhackers exist in the woods, who shoot unsuspecting stragglers, and it would therefore be unsafe that Lawley and I should travel alone. General Longstreet is an Alabamian[19]—a thickset, determined-looking man, forty-three years of age. He was an infantry Major in the old army, and now commands the 1st *corps d'armée*. He is never far from General Lee, who relies very much upon his judgment. By the soldiers he is invariably spoken of as "the best fighter in the whole army." Whilst speaking of entering upon the enemy's soil, he said to me, that although it might be fair, in just retaliation, *to apply the torch,* yet that doing so would demoralize the army and ruin its now excellent discipline. Private property is to be therefore rigidly protected.

At 7 A.M. I returned with an orderly (or courier, as they are called) to the farm-house in which I had left Lawley; and after seeing all arranged satisfactorily about the ambulance, I rode slowly on to rejoin General Longstreet, near Chambersburg, which is a Pennsylvanian town, distant twenty-two miles from Hagerstown. I was with McLaws's division, and observed that the moment they entered Pennsylvania, the troops opened the fences and enlarged the road about twenty yards on each side, which enabled the wagons and themselves to proceed together. This is the only damage I saw done by the Confederates. This part of Pennsylvania is very flourishing, highly cultivated, and, in comparison with the Southern States, thickly peopled. But all the cattle and horses having been seized by Ewell, farm-labor had now come to a complete standstill.

In passing through Greencastle we found all the houses and windows shut up, the natives in their Sunday clothes standing at their doors regarding the troops in a very un-

---

[19] Born in South Carolina and reared during his early childhood in Georgia, Longstreet spent his later youth in Alabama and was appointed to West Point from that state.

Lt. Gen. James Longstreet

friendly manner. I saw no straggling into the houses, nor were any of the inhabitants disturbed or annoyed by the soldiers. Sentries were placed at the doors of many of the best houses, to prevent any officer or soldier from getting in on any pretence.

I entered Chambersburg at 6 P.M. This is a town of some size and importance. All its houses were shut up; but the natives were in the streets, or at the upper windows, looking in a scowling and bewildered manner at the Confederate troops, who were marching gayly past to the tune of Dixie's Land. The women (many of whom were pretty and well dressed) were particularly sour and disagreeable in their remarks. I heard one of them say, "Look at Pharaoh's army going to the Red Sea." Others were pointing and laughing at Hood's ragged Jacks, who were passing at the time. This division, well known for its fighting qualities, is composed of Texans, Alabamians, and Arkansians, and they certainly are a queer lot to look at.[20] They carry less than any other troops; many of them have only got an old piece of carpet or rug as baggage; many have discarded their shoes in the mud; all are ragged and dirty, but full of good-humor and confidence in themselves and in their general, Hood. They answered the numerous taunts of the Chambersburg ladies with cheers and laughter. One female had seen fit to adorn her ample bosom with a huge Yankee flag, and she stood at the door of her house, her countenance expressing the greatest contempt for the barefooted Rebs; several companies passed her without taking any notice; but at length a Texan gravely remarked, "Take care, madam, for Hood's boys are great at storming breast-works when the Yankee colors is on them." After this speech the patriotic lady beat a precipitate retreat.

Sentries were placed at the doors of all the principal houses, and the town was cleared of all but the military pass-

[20] Maj. Gen. John Bell Hood, a native of Kentucky and for much of his life a resident of Texas, headed a division containing one brigade of Alabama troops, two brigades of Georgians, and one brigade, the famous unit Hood himself had once led, comprised of three regiments of Texans and one of Arkansans.

ing through or on duty. Some of the troops marched straight through the town, and bivouacked on the Carlisle road. Others turned off to the right, and occupied the Gettysburg turnpike. I found Generals Lee and Longstreet encamped on the latter road, three-quarters of a mile from the town.

General Longstreet and his Staff at once received me into their mess, and I was introduced to Major Fairfax, Major Latrobe, and Captain Rogers of his personal Staff; also to Major Moses, the Chief Commissary, whose tent I am ·to share. He is the most jovial, amusing, clever son of Israel I ever had the good fortune to meet. The other officers of Longstreet's Headquarter Staff are Colonel Sorrel, Lieutenant-colonel Manning (ordnance officer), Major Walton, Captain Goree, and Major Clarke, all excellent good fellows, and most hospitable.*[21]

*Having lived at the headquarters of all the principal Confederate Generals, I am able to affirm that the relation between their Staffs and themselves, and the way the duty is carried on, is very similar to what it is in the British army. All the Generals—Johnston, Bragg, Polk, Hardee, Longstreet, and Lee—are thorough soldiers, and their Staffs are composed of gentlemen of position and education, who have now been trained into excellent and zealous Staff officers.[22]

[21] The roster of Longstreet's staff included Maj. John Fairfax, a member of a prominent Virginia family; Maj. Osmun Latrobe, a young man from one of Maryland's leading families; Captain H. J. Rogers; Maj. Raphael J. Moses, a South Carolina lawyer in his early fifties; Lt. Col. Gilbert Moxley Sorrel of South Carolina, whose Recollections of a Confederate Staff Officer (New York and Washington: The Neale Publishing Company, 1905; reprinted several times) is among the most frequently quoted sources on the Army of Northern Virginia; Lt. Col. Peyton T. Manning, an Alabamian in his mid-twenties who, as ordnance officer, looked after the arms and ammunition in Longstreet's corps; Maj. Thomas Walton, another Alabamian; Maj. Thomas Jewett Goree, a lawyer born in Alabama but long a resident of Texas, who served with Longstreet from the beginning to the end of the war; and Maj. John J. Clarke, a civil engineer from Petersburg, Virginia. For Sorrel's discussion of Fremantle, see Recollections of a Confederate Staff Officer, pp. 160–61.

[22] Earlier in his journey, Fremantle had been with Gen. Joseph Eggleston Johnston, a Virginian in command of Confederate forces between the Appalachians and the Mississippi River; Gen. Braxton Bragg, a native of North Carolina who commanded the Army of Tennessee; and Lt. Gen. William Joseph Hardee, who led a corps of Bragg's army.

Lawley is to live with three doctors on the Headquarter Staff: their names are Cullen, Barksdale, and Maury; they form a jolly trio, and live much more luxuriously than their generals.[23]

Major Moses tells me that his orders are to open the stores in Chambersburg by force, and seize all that is wanted for the army in a regular and official manner, giving in return its value in Confederate money on a receipt. The storekeepers have doubtless sent away their most valuable goods on the approach of the Confederate army. Much also has been already seized by Ewell, who passed through nearly a week ago. But Moses was much elated at having already discovered a large supply of excellent felt hats, hidden away in a cellar, which he "annexed" at once.

I was told this evening the numbers which have crossed the Potomac, and also the number of pieces of artillery. There is a large train of ammunition; for if the army advances any deeper into the enemy's country, General Lee cannot expect to keep his communications open to the rear; and as the Staff officers say, "In every battle we fight we must capture as much ammunition as we use." This necessity, however, does not seem to disturb them, as it has hitherto been their regular style of doing business.

Ewell, after the capture of Winchester, had advanced rapidly into Pennsylvania, and has already sent back great quantities of horses, mules, wagons, beeves, and other necessaries; he is now at or beyond Carlisle, laying the country under contribution, and making Pennsylvania support the war, instead of poor, used-up, and worn-out Virginia. The corps of Generals A. P. Hill and Longstreet are now near this place, all full of confidence and in high spirits.

28th June (Sunday).—No officer or soldier under the rank of a general is allowed into Chambersburg without a

[23] The surgeons were J. S. D. "Dorsey" Cullen, who stood with Sorrel, Moses, Fairfax, Goree, Latrobe, and Manning within Longstreet's inner circle; Randolph Barksdale, medical inspector for the First Corps serving under Cullen; and Thomas F. Maury.

Lt. Gen. Ambrose Powell Hill

special order from General Lee, which he is very chary of giving; and I hear of officers of rank being refused this pass.

Moses proceeded into town at 11 A.M., with an official requisition for three days' rations for the whole army in this neighborhood. These rations he is to seize by force, if not voluntarily supplied.

I was introduced to General Hood this morning; he is a tall, thin, wiry-looking man, with a grave face and a light-colored beard, thirty-three years old, and is accounted one of the best and most promising officers in the army. By his Texan and Alabamian troops he is adored; he formerly commanded the Texan brigade, but has now been promoted to the command of a division. His troops are accused of being a wild set, and difficult to manage; and it is the great object of the chiefs to check their innate plundering propensities by every means in their power.

I went into Chambersburg at noon, and found Lawley ensconced in the Franklin Hotel. Both he and I had much difficulty in getting into that establishment—the doors being locked, and only opened with the greatest caution. Lawley had had a most painful journey in the ambulance yesterday, and was much exhausted. No one in the hotel would take the slightest notice of him, and all scowled at me in a most disagreeable manner. Half-a-dozen Pennsylvanian viragos surrounded and assailed me with their united tongues to a deafening degree. Nor would they believe me when I told them I was an English spectator and a non-combatant: they said I must be either a Rebel or a Yankee—by which expression I learned for the first time that the term Yankee is as much used as a reproach in Pennsylvania as in the South. The sight of gold, which I exchanged for their greenbacks, brought about a change, and by degrees they became quite affable. They seemed very ignorant, and confused Texans with Mexicans.

After leaving Lawley pretty comfortable, I walked about the town and witnessed the pressing operations of Moses and his myrmidons. Neither the Mayor nor the corporation were to be found anywhere, nor were the keys of the principal stores forthcoming until Moses began to apply the axe. The citizens were lolling about the streets in a listless manner, and showing no great signs of discontent. They had left to their women the task of resisting the commissaries—a duty which they were fully competent to perform. No soldiers but those on duty were visible in the streets.

In the evening I called again to see Lawley, and found in his room an Austrian officer, in the full uniform of the Hungarian hussars.[24] He had got a year's leave of absence, and has just succeeded in crossing the Potomac, though not without much trouble and difficulty. When he stated his intention of wearing his uniform, I explained to him the invariable custom of the Confederate soldiers, of never allowing the smallest peculiarity of dress or appearance to pass without a torrent of jokes, which, however good-humored, ended in becoming rather monotonous.

I returned to camp at 6 P.M. Major Moses did not get back till very late, much depressed at the ill-success of his mission. He had searched all day most indefatigably, and had endured much contumely from the Union ladies, who called him "a thievish little rebel scoundrel," and other opprobrious epithets. But this did not annoy him so much as the manner in which every thing he wanted had been sent away or hidden in private houses, which he was not allowed by General Lee's order to search. He had only managed to secure a quantity of molasses, sugar, and whiskey. Poor Moses was thoroughly exhausted; but he endured the chaff of his brother officers with much good-humor, and they made him continually repeat the different names he had been called. He said that at first the women refused his Confederate "trash" with great

---

[24] The "Austrian" was Capt. FitzGerald Ross, an English cavalry officer serving with the Austrian Hussars who spent much of 1863 and the first part of 1864 in the Confederacy. Ross's *Cities and Camps of the Confederate States* (first published in England in 1865 and reprinted by the University of Illinois Press in 1958) discusses many of the same events Fremantle describes.

scorn, but they ended in being very particular about the odd cents.

29th June (Monday).—We are still at Chambersburg. Lee has issued a remarkably good order on non-retaliation, which is generally well received; but I have heard of complaints from fire-eaters, who want vengeance for their wrongs; and when one considers the numbers of officers and soldiers with this army who have been totally ruined by the devastations of Northern troops, one cannot be much surprised at this feeling.[25]

I went into Chambersburg again, and witnessed the singular good behavior of the troops towards the citizens. I heard soldiers saying to one another, that they did not like being in a town in which they were very naturally detested. To any one who has seen *as I have* the ravages of the Northern troops in Southern towns, this forbearance seems most commendable and surprising. Yet these Pennsylvanian Dutch* don't seem the least thankful, and really appear to be unaware that their own troops have been for two years treating Southern towns with ten times more harshness. They are the most unpatriotic people I ever saw, and openly state that they don't care which side wins, provided they are left alone. They abuse Lincoln tremendously.

Of course, in such a large army as this there must be many instances of bad characters, who are always ready to plunder and pillage whenever they can do so without being caught: the stragglers, also, who remain behind when the

---

*This part of Pennsylvania is much peopled with the descendants of Germans, who speak an unintelligible language.

[25] Lee's General Orders No. 73, issued from army headquarters at Chambersburg on June 27, 1863, closed with an admonition to the officers and soldiers in the army: "The commanding general therefore earnestly exhorts the troops to abstain with most scrupulous care from unnecessary or wanton injury to private property, and he enjoins upon all officers to arrest and bring to summary punishment all who shall in any way offend against the orders on this subject."

army has left, will doubtless do much harm. It is impossible to prevent this; but every thing that can be done is done to protect private property and non-combatants, and I can say, from my own observation, with wonderful success. I hear instances, however, in which soldiers, meeting well-dressed citizens, have made a "long arm" and changed hats, much to the disgust of the latter, who are still more annoyed when an exchange of boots is also proposed: their superfine broadcloth is never in any danger.

General Longstreet is generally a particularly taciturn man; but this evening he and I had a long talk about Texas, where he had been quartered a long time. He remembered many people whom I had met quite well, and was much amused by the description of my travels through that country. I complimented him upon the manner in which the Confederate sentries do their duty, and said that they were quite as strict as, and ten times more polite than, regular soldiers. He replied, laughing, that a sentry, after refusing you leave to enter a camp, might very likely, if properly asked, show you another way in, by which you might avoid meeting a sentry at all.

I saw General Pendleton[26] and General Pickett to-day. Pendleton is Chief of Artillery to the army, and was a West-Pointer; but in more peaceable times he fills the post of Episcopal clergyman in Lexington, Virginia. Unlike General Polk,[27] he unites the military and clerical professions together, and continues to preach whenever he gets a chance. On these occasions he wears a surplice over his uniform.

General Pickett commands one of the divisions in Longstreet's corps.* He wears his hair in long ringlets, and is

---

*McLaws, Hood, and Pickett, are the three divisional commanders or major-generals in Longstreet's *corps d'armée.*

[26] Brig. Gen. William Nelson Pendleton of Virginia.

[27] Before he reached Virginia, Fremantle had spent considerable time with Lt. Gen. Leonidas Polk, a native of North Carolina and former Episcopal Ministry Bishop of the Southwest who served as a corps commander in the Confederate Army of Tennessee.

altogether rather a desperate looking character. He is the officer who, as Captain Pickett of the U.S. army, figured in the difficulty between the British and United States in the San Juan Island affair, under General Harney, four or five years ago.[28]

30th June (Tuesday).—This morning, before marching from Chambersburg, General Longstreet introduced me to the Commander-in-chief. General Lee is, almost without exception, the handsomest man of his age I ever saw. He is fifty-six years old, tall, broad-shouldered, very well made, well set up—a thorough soldier in appearance; and his manners are most courteous and full of dignity. He is a perfect gentleman in every respect. I imagine no man has so few enemies, or is so universally esteemed. Throughout the South, all agree in pronouncing him to be as near perfection as a man can be. He has none of the small vices, such as smoking, drinking, chewing, or swearing, and his bitterest enemy never accused him of any of the greater ones. He generally wears a well-worn long gray jacket, a high black felt hat, and blue trousers tucked into his Wellington boots. I never saw him carry arms;* and the only mark of his military rank are the three stars on his collar.[29] He rides a handsome horse, which is extremely well groomed. He himself is very neat in his dress

---

*I never saw either Lee or Longstreet carry arms. A. P. Hill generally wears a sword.

[28] Brig. Gen. William Selby Harney, commander of the Department of Oregon, and then-Captain Pickett were involved in a late-antebellum dispute between the United States and Great Britain over San Juan Island in Puget Sound. In 1859, Pickett and a few dozen American soldiers under his charge occupied the island, resisted British pressure to abandon their position, and eventually took part in a joint occupation of San Juan.

[29] Lee wore the three stars of a colonel rather than the stars and wreath prescribed for general officers by Confederate regulations. For a discussion of why he did so, see Edward D. C. Campbell, "R. E. Lee, Confederate Insignia, and the Perception of Rank," *The Virginia Magazine of History and Biography* 98 (April 1990):261–90.

Maj. Gen. George Edward Pickett

and person, and in the most arduous marches he always looks smart and clean.†

In the old army he was always considered one of its best officers; and at the outbreak of these troubles, he was Lieutenant-colonel of the 2d Cavalry.[30] He was a rich man, but his fine estate was one of the first to fall into the enemy's hands.[31] I believe he has never slept in a house since he has commanded the Virginian army, and he invariably declines all offers of hospitality, for fear the person offering it may afterwards get into trouble for having sheltered the Rebel General. The relations between him and Longstreet are quite touching—they are almost always together. Longstreet's corps complain of this sometimes, as they say that they seldom get a chance of detached service, which falls to the lot of Ewell. It is impossible to please Longstreet more than by praising Lee. I believe these two Generals to be as little ambitious and as thoroughly unselfish as any men in the world. Both long for a successful termination of the war, in order that they may retire into obscurity. Stonewall Jackson (until his death the third in command of their army) was just such another simple-minded servant of his country. It is understood that General Lee is a religious man, though not so demonstrative in that respect as Jackson; and, unlike his late brother in arms, he is a member of the Church of England. His only faults, so far as I can learn, arise from his excessive amiability.

†I observed this during the three days' fighting at Gettysburg, and in the retreat afterwards, when every one else looked, and was, extremely dirty.

[30] On March 16, 1861, slightly more than a month before he resigned from the United States army, Lee had been promoted to colonel and given command of the 1st Cavalry.

[31] Fremantle refers to the estate at Arlington, Virginia, just across the Potomac River from Washington, D.C. Upon the death of her father, George Washington Parke Custis, in the fall of 1857, Lee's wife Mary Custis Lee received a life interest in this property. Custis's will mandated that when Mrs. Lee died the estate would pass in fee to George Washington Custis Lee, the eldest son of Robert and Mary.

Gen. R. E. Lee

Some Texan soldiers were sent this morning into Chambersburg to destroy a number of barrels of excellent whiskey, which could not be carried away. This was a pretty good trial for their discipline, and they did think it rather hard lines that the only time they had been allowed into the enemy's town was for the purpose of destroying their beloved whiskey. However, they did their duty like good soldiers.

We marched six miles on the road towards Gettysburg, and encamped at a village called (I think) Greenwood. I rode Lawley's old horse, he and the Austrian using the doctor's ambulance. In the evening General Longstreet told me that he had just received intelligence that Hooker had been disrated, and that Meade was appointed in his place. Of course he knew both of them in the old army, and he says that Meade is an honorable and respectable man, though not, perhaps, so bold as Hooker.

I had a long talk with many officers about the approaching battle, which evidently cannot now be delayed long, and will take place on this road instead of in the direction of Harrisburg, as we had supposed. Ewell, who has laid York as well as Carlisle under contribution, has been ordered to reunite. Every one, of course, speaks with confidence. I remarked that it would be a good thing for them if on this occasion they had cavalry to follow up the broken infantry in the event of their succeeding in beating them. But to my surprise they all spoke of their cavalry as not efficient for that purpose. In fact, Stuart's men, though excellent at making raids, capturing wagons and stores, and cutting off communications, seem to have no idea of charging infantry under any circumstances. Unlike the cavalry with Bragg's army, they wear swords, but seem to have little idea of using them— they hanker after their carbines and revolvers. They constantly ride with their swords between their left leg and the saddle, which has a very funny appearance; but their horses are generally good, and they ride well. The infantry and artillery of this army don't seem to respect the cavalry very much, and often jeer at them.[32] I was forced to abandon my horse here, as he was now lame in three legs, besides having a very sore back.

1st July (Wednesday).—We did not leave our camp till noon, as nearly all General Hill's corps had to pass our quarters on its march towards Gettysburg. One division of Ewell's also had to join in a little beyond Greenwood, and Longstreet's corps had to bring up the rear. During the morning I made the acquaintance of Colonel Walton, who used to command the well-known Washington Artillery, but he is now chief of artillery to Longstreet's *corps d'armée*.[33] He is a big man, *ci-devant* auctioneer in New Orleans, and I understand he pines to return to his hammer.

Soon after starting we got into a pass in the South Mountain, a continuation, I believe, of the Blue Ridge range, which is broken by the Potomac at Harper's Ferry. The scenery through the pass is very fine. The first troops, alongside of whom we rode, belonged to Johnson's[34] division of Ewell's corps. Among them I saw, for the first time, the celebrated "Stonewall" Brigade, formerly commanded by Jackson. In appearance the men differ little from other Confeder-

[32] Fremantle was correct in observing that the infantrymen and artillerists in Lee's army often deprecated the cavalry as a fighting arm of the service; the infantry often asked, "Whoever saw a dead cavalryman?" But Fremantle did not understand that the advent of the rifle musket rendered hopeless a cavalry charge against infantry. Stuart's cavalry generally carried out its assigned missions very capably.

[33] Col. James Burdge Walton, born in New Jersey but a longtime resident of New Orleans, served as titular head of Longstreet's artillery. On the battlefield at Gettysburg and elsewhere, however, effective command of the First Corps guns rested with the much younger and more gifted Col. Edward Porter Alexander of Georgia. Alexander eventually succeeded Walton as Longstreet's chief gunner and ended the war as a brigadier general.

[34] Maj. Gen. Edward "Allegheny" Johnson of Virginia led a division of two brigades from Virginia, one from Louisiana, and one with units from Virginia, Maryland, and North Carolina.

ate soldiers, except, perhaps, that the brigade contains more elderly men and fewer boys. All (except, I think, one regiment) are Virginians.[35] As they have nearly always been on detached duty, few of them knew General Longstreet, except by reputation. Numbers of them asked me whether the General in front was Longstreet; and when I answered in the affirmative, many would run on a hundred yards in order to take a good look at him. This I take to be an immense compliment from any soldier on a long march.

At 2 P.M. firing became distinctly audible in our front, but although it increased as we progressed, it did not seem to be very heavy.

A spy who was with us insisted upon there being "a pretty tidy bunch of *blue-bellies* in or near Gettysburg," and he declared that he was in their society three days ago.

After passing Johnson's division, we came up to a Florida brigade, which is now in Hill's corps; but as it had formerly served under Longstreet, the men knew him well. Some of them (after the General had passed) called out to their comrades, "Look out for work now, boys, for here's the old bull-dog again."

At 3 P.M. we began to meet wounded men coming to the rear, and the number of these soon increased most rapidly, some hobbling alone, others on stretchers carried by the ambulance corps, and others in the ambulance wagons. Many of the latter were stripped nearly naked, and displayed very bad wounds. This spectacle, so revolting to a person unaccustomed to such sights, produced no impression whatever upon the advancing troops, who certainly go under fire with the most perfect nonchalance. They show no enthusiasm or excitement, but the most complete indifference. This is the effect of two years' almost uninterrupted fighting.

We now began to meet Yankee prisoners coming to the rear in considerable numbers. Many of them were wounded,

---

[35] The Stonewall Brigade consisted of the 2nd, 4th, 5th, 27th, and 33rd regiments of Virginia infantry.

but they seemed already to be on excellent terms with their captors, with whom they had commenced swapping canteens, tobacco, &c. Among them was a Pennsylvanian Colonel, a miserable object from a wound in his face. In answer to a question, I heard one of them remark, with a laugh, "We're pretty nigh whipped already." We next came to a Confederate soldier carrying a Yankee color, belonging, I think, to a Pennsylvania regiment, which he told us he had just captured.

At 4:30 P.M. we came in sight of Gettysburg, and joined General Lee and General Hill, who were on the top of one of the ridges which form the peculiar feature of the country round Gettysburg.[36] We could see the enemy retreating up one of the opposite ridges, pursued by the Confederates with loud yells. The position into which the enemy had been driven was evidently a strong one. His right appeared to rest on a cemetery, on the top of a high ridge to the right of Gettysburg, as we looked at it.

General Hill now came up and told me he had been very unwell all day, and in fact he looks very delicate. He said he had had two of his divisions engaged, and had driven the enemy four miles into his present position, capturing a great many prisoners, some cannon, and some colors. He said, however, that the Yankees had fought with a determination unusual to them. He pointed out a railway cutting, in which they had made a good stand; also, a field in the centre of which he had seen a man plant the regimental color, round which the regiment had fought for some time with much obstinacy, and when at last it was obliged to retreat, the colorbearer retired last of all, turning round every now and then to shake his fist at the advancing rebels. General Hill said he felt quite sorry when he saw this gallant Yankee meet his doom.

General Ewell had come up at 3:30, on the enemy's right (with part of his corps), and completed his discomfiture. General Reynolds, one of the best Yankee generals, was

[36] Fremantle joined Lee and Hill on Seminary Ridge.

reported killed. Whilst we were talking, a message arrived from General Ewell, requesting Hill to press the enemy in the front, whilst he performed the same operation on his right. The pressure was accordingly applied in a mild degree, but the enemy were too strongly posted, and it was too late in the evening for a regular attack.[37] The town of Gettysburg was now occupied by Ewell, and was full of Yankee dead and wounded. I climbed up a tree in the most commanding place I could find, and could form a pretty good general idea of the enemy's position, although the tops of the ridges being covered with pine-woods, it was very difficult to see any thing of the troops concealed in them. The firing ceased about dark, at which time I rode back with General Longstreet and his Staff to his headquarters at Cashtown, a little village eight miles from Gettysburg. At that time troops were pouring along the road, and were being marched towards the position they are to occupy to-morrow.

In the fight to-day nearly 6,000 prisoners had been taken, and 10 guns. About 20,000 men must have been on the field on the Confederate side. The enemy had two *corps d'armée* engaged. All the prisoners belong, I think, to the 1st and 11th corps. This day's work is called a "brisk little scurry," and all anticipate a "big battle" to-morrow.

I observed that the artillerymen in charge of the horses dig themselves little holes like graves, throwing up the earth at the upper end. They ensconce themselves in these holes when under fire.

At supper this evening, General Longstreet spoke of the enemy's position as being "very formidable." He also said that they would doubtless intrench themselves strongly during the night.* The Staff officers spoke of the battle as a cer-

---

*I have the best reason for supposing that the fight came off prematurely, and that neither Lee nor Longstreet intended that it should have begun that day. I also think that their plans were deranged by the events of the first.

[37] The failure of Confederate forces to press their advantage on July 1 subsequently generated a great deal of controversy. For a review of this literature, see the essays by Alan T. Nolan and Gary W. Gallagher in Gallagher, ed., *The First Day at Gettysburg*.

tainty, and the universal feeling in the army was one of pro-
found contempt for an enemy whom they have beaten so
constantly, and under so many disadvantages.

2d July (Thursday).—We all got up at 3:30 A.M., and
breakfasted a little before daylight. Lawley insisted on riding,
notwithstanding his illness. Captain —— and I were in a
dilemma for horses; but I was accommodated by Major
Clarke (of this Staff), whilst the stout Austrian was mounted
by Major Walton. The Austrian, in spite of the early hour,
had shaved his cheeks and *ciréd* his mustaches as beautifully
as if he was on parade at Vienna.

Colonel Sorrel, the Austrian, and I arrived at 5 A.M. at
the same commanding position we were on yesterday, and I
climbed up a tree in company with Captain Scheibert of the
Prussian army. Just below us were seated Generals Lee, Hill,
Longstreet, and Hood, in consultation—the two latter assisting their deliberations by the truly American custom of *whit-
tling* sticks. General Heth[38] was also present; he was wounded
in the head yesterday, and although not allowed to command
his brigade, he insists upon coming to the field.

At 7 A.M. I rode over part of the ground with General
Longstreet, and saw him disposing of McLaws's division for
to-day's fight. The enemy occupied a series of high ridges, the
tops of which were covered with trees, but the intervening
valleys between their ridges and ours were mostly open, and
partly under cultivation. The cemetery was on their right, and
their left appeared to rest upon a high rocky hill.[39] The
enemy's forces, which were now supposed to comprise nearly
the whole Potomac army, were concentrated into a space
apparently not more than a couple of miles in length. The
Confederates inclosed them in a sort of semicircle, and the
extreme extent of our position must have been from five to
six miles at least. Ewell was on our left; his headquarters in a

[38] Maj. Gen. Henry Heth of Virginia, a division commander in Hill's
Third Corps.
[39] Fremantle could have been describing as a "high rocky hill" either
Little Round Top or Round Top.

Union Breastworks
at Gettysburg

church (with a high cupola) at Gettysburg; Hill in the centre; and Longstreet on the right. Our ridges were also covered with pine-woods at the tops, and generally on the rear slopes. The artillery of both sides confronted each other at the edges of these belts of trees, the troops being completely hidden. The enemy was evidently intrenched, but the Southerners had not broken ground at all. A dead silence reigned till 4:45 P.M., and no one would have imagined that such masses of men and such a powerful artillery were about to commence the work of destruction at that hour.

Only two divisions of Longstreet were present to-day— viz., McLaws's and Hood's—Pickett being still in the rear. As the whole morning was evidently to be occupied in disposing the troops for the attack,[40] I rode to the extreme right with Colonel Manning and Major Walton, where we ate quantities of cherries, and got a feed of corn for our horses. We also bathed in a small stream, but not without some trepidation on my part, for we were almost beyond the lines, and were exposed to the enemy's cavalry.

At 1 P.M. I met a quantity of Yankee prisoners who had been picked up straggling. They told me they belonged to Sickles's corps (3d, I think), and had arrived from Emmitsburg during the night. About this time skirmishing began along part of the line, but not heavily.

At 2 P.M. General Longstreet advised me, if I wished to have a good view of the battle, to return to my tree of yester-

[40] Longstreet's behavior on July 2 became the focus of a huge controversial literature. Many former Confederates and later writers accused him of delay in getting his corps into position to assault the Federal army. For the definitive unfavorable assessment, see Robert K. Krick, " 'If Longstreet . . . Says So, It Is Most Likely Not True': James Longstreet and the Second Day at Gettysburg," in Gallagher, ed., *The Second Day at Gettysburg;* for more favorable evaluations, see Jeffry D. Wert's *General James Longstreet: The Confederacy's Most Controversial Soldier, A Biography* (New York: Simon & Schuster, 1993) and William Garrett Piston's *Lee's Tarnished Lieutenant: General James Longstreet and His Place in Southern History* (Athens, Ga.: University of Georgia Press, 1987).

day. I did so, and remained there with Lawley and Captain Scheibert during the rest of the afternoon. But until 4:45 P.M. all was profoundly still, and we began to doubt whether a fight was coming off to-day at all. At that time, however, Longstreet suddenly commenced a heavy cannonade on the right. Ewell immediately took it up on the left. The enemy replied with at least equal fury, and in a few moments the firing along the whole line was as heavy as it is possible to conceive. A dense smoke arose for six miles; there was little wind to drive it away, and the air seemed full of shells—each of which appeared to have a different style of going, and to make a different noise from the others. The ordnance on both sides is of a very varied description. Every now and then a caisson would blow up—if a Federal one, a Confederate yell would immediately follow. The Southern troops, when charging, or to express their delight, always yell in a manner peculiar to themselves. The Yankee cheer is much more like ours; but the Confederate officers declare that the rebel yell has a particular merit, and always produces a salutary and useful effect upon their adversaries. A corps is sometimes spoken of as a "good yelling regiment."[41]

So soon as the firing began, General Lee joined Hill just below our tree, and he remained there nearly all the time, looking through his field-glass—sometimes talking to Hill and sometimes to Colonel Long[42] of his Staff. But generally he sat quite alone on the stump of a tree. What I remarked especially was, that during the whole time the firing continued, he only sent one message, and only received one report. It is evidently his system to arrange the plan thoroughly with

[41] Many witnesses commented on the differences between the Union and the Confederate cheer—the northerners having a deeper, more rhythmic series of "huzzas," the southerners having their famous "rebel yell," a less disciplined, higher-pitched shout sometimes likened to a fox-hunter's cry.

[42] Before being promoted to brigadier general and placed in command of the Second Corps artillery in September 1863, Col. Armistead Lindsay Long of Virginia served as Lee's military secretary.

the three corps commanders, and then leave to them the duty of modifying and carrying it out to the best of their abilities.

When the cannonade was at its height, a Confederate band of music, between the cemetery and ourselves, began to play polkas and waltzes, which sounded very curious, accompanied by the hissing and bursting of the shells.

At 5:45 all became comparatively quiet on our left and in the cemetery; but volleys of musketry on the right told us that Longstreet's infantry were advancing, and the onward progress of the smoke showed that he was progressing favorably; but about 6:30 there seemed to be a check, and even a slight retrograde movement. Soon after 7, General Lee got a report by signal from Longstreet to say *"we are doing well."* A little before dark the firing dropped off in every direction, and soon ceased altogether. We then received intelligence that Longstreet had carried every thing before him for some time, capturing several batteries, and driving the enemy from his positions; but when Hill's Florida brigade and some other troops gave way, he was forced to abandon a small portion of the ground he had won, together with all the captured guns, except three. His troops, however, bivouacked during the night on ground occupied by the enemy this morning.

Every one deplores that Longstreet *will* expose himself in such a reckless manner. To-day he led a Georgian regiment in a charge against a battery, hat in hand, and in front of everybody. General Barksdale was killed and Semmes mortally wounded; but the most serious loss was that of General Hood, who was badly wounded in the arm early in the day. I heard that his Texans are in despair. Lawley and I rode back to the General's camp, which had been moved to within a mile of the scene of action. Longstreet, however, with most of his Staff, bivouacked on the field.

Major Fairfax arrived at about 10 P.M. in a very bad humor. He had under his charge about 1,000 to 1,500 Yankee prisoners who had been taken to-day; among them a general, whom I heard one of his men accusing of having been "so G—d d—d drunk that he had turned his guns upon his own men." But, on the other hand, the accuser was such a thundering blackguard, and proposed taking such a variety of oaths in order to escape from the U.S. army, that he is not worthy of much credit. A large train of horses and mules, &c., arrived to-day, sent in by General Stuart, and captured, it is understood, by his cavalry, which had penetrated to within 6 miles of Washington.

3d July (Friday).—At 6 A.M. I rode to the field with Colonel Manning, and went over that portion of the ground which, after a fierce contest, had been won from the enemy yesterday evening. The dead were being buried, but great numbers were still lying about; also many mortally wounded, for whom nothing could be done. Amongst the latter were a number of Yankees dressed in bad imitations of the Zouave costume.[43] They opened their glazed eyes as I rode past in a painfully imploring manner.

We joined Generals Lee and Longstreet's Staff: they were reconnoitring and making preparations for renewing the attack. As we formed a pretty large party, we often drew upon ourselves the attention of the hostile sharpshooters, and were two or three times favored with a shell. One of these shells set a brick building on fire which was situated between the lines. This building was filled with wounded, principally Yankees, who, I am afraid, must have perished miserably in the flames. Colonel Sorrel had been slightly wounded yesterday, but still did duty. Major Walton's horse was killed, but there were no other casualties amongst my particular friends.

The plan of yesterday's attack seems to have been very simple—first a heavy cannonade all along the line, followed by an advance of Longstreet's two divisions and part of Hill's corps. In consequence of the enemy's having been driven back some distance, Longstreet's corps (part of it) was in a much more forward situation than yesterday. But the range

---

[43] Several Civil War units on both sides wore uniforms patterned on those of the French Army Zouaves. Typical components of this dress included white leggings, baggy red pants, a blue jacket, and a red fez.

of heights to be gained was still most formidable, and evidently strongly intrenched.

The distance between the Confederate guns and the Yankee position—*i.e.*, between the woods crowning the opposite ridges—was at least a mile—quite open, gently undulating, and exposed to artillery the whole distance. This was the ground which had to be crossed in to-day's attack. Pickett's division, which had just come up, was to bear the brunt in Longstreet's attack, together with Heth and Pettigrew in Hill's corps. Pickett's division was a weak one (under 5,000), owing to the absence of two brigades.[44]

At noon all Longstreet's dispositions were made; his troops for attack were deployed into line, and lying down in the woods; his batteries were ready to open. The general then dismounted and went to sleep for a short time. The Austrian officer and I now rode off to get, if possible, into some commanding position from whence we could see the whole thing without being exposed to the tremendous fire which was about to commence. After riding about for half an hour without being able to discover so desirable a situation, we determined to make for the cupola, near Gettysburg, Ewell's headquarters. Just before we reached the entrance to the town, the cannonade opened with a fury which surpassed even that of yesterday.

Soon after passing through the toll-gate at the entrance of Gettysburg, we found that we had got into a heavy crossfire; shells both Federal and Confederate passing over our

---

[44] The ridges mentioned by Fremantle are Seminary Ridge, occupied by Confederate troops, and Cemetery Ridge, where Union defenders awaited the southern assault. The distance between the two is approximately seven-tenths of a mile. On July 3, Brig. Gen. James Johnston Pettigrew of North Carolina commanded the division of Henry Heth, who had been wounded on the first day of the battle. William Dorsey Pender also had been wounded, and his division passed on July 3 to Maj. Gen. Isaac Ridgeway Trimble, a native of Virginia. In the three brigades of Pickett's division, the four brigades under Pettigrew, and two brigades under Trimble (two of the brigades in Pendor's division did not participate in the charge), the assaulting column numbered approximately 13,000 men.

heads with great frequency. At length two shrapnel shells burst quite close to us, and a ball from one of them hit the officer who was conducting us. We then turned round and changed our views with regard to the cupola—the fire of one side being bad enough, but preferable to that of both sides. A small boy of twelve years was riding with us at the time: this urchin took a diabolical interest in the bursting of the shells, and screamed with delight when he saw them take effect. I never saw this boy again, or found out who he was.

The road at Gettysburg was lined with Yankee dead, and as they had been killed on the 1st, the poor fellows had already begun to be very offensive. We then returned to the hill I was on yesterday. But finding that, to see the actual fighting, it was absolutely necessary to go into the thick of the thing, I determined to make my way to General Longstreet. It was then about 2:30. After passing General Lee and his Staff, I rode on through the woods in the direction in which I had left Longstreet. I soon began to meet many wounded men returning from the front; many of them asked in piteous tones the way to a doctor or an ambulance. The further I got, the greater became the number of the wounded. At last I came to a perfect stream of them flocking through the woods in numbers as great as the crowd in Oxford-street in the middle of the day. Some were walking alone on crutches composed of two rifles, others were supported by men less badly wounded than themselves, and others were carried on stretchers by the ambulance corps; but in no case did I see a sound man helping the wounded to the rear, unless he carried the red badge of the ambulance corps. They were still under a heavy fire; the shells were continually bringing down great limbs of trees, and carrying further destruction amongst this melancholy procession. I saw all this in much less time than it takes to write it, and although astonished to meet such vast numbers of wounded, I had not seen *enough* to give me any idea of the real extent of the mischief.

When I got close up to General Longstreet, I saw one of his regiments advancing through the woods in good order;

so, thinking I was just in time to see the attack, I remarked to the General that *"I wouldn't have missed this for any thing."* Longstreet was seated at the top of a snake fence at the edge of the wood, and looking perfectly calm and imperturbed. He replied, laughing, *"The devil you wouldn't! I would like to have missed it very much; we've attacked and been repulsed: look there!"* [45]

For the first time I then had a view of the open space between the two positions, and saw it covered with Confederates slowly and sulkily returning towards us in small broken parties, under a heavy fire of artillery. But the fire where we were was not so bad as further to the rear; for although the air seemed alive with shell, yet the greater number burst behind us.

The General told me that Pickett's division had succeeded in carrying the enemy's position and capturing his guns, but after remaining there twenty minutes, it had been forced to retire, on the retreat of Heth and Pettigrew on its left. No person could have been more calm or self-possessed than General Longstreet under these trying circumstances, aggravated as they now were by the movements of the enemy, who began to show a strong disposition to advance. I could now thoroughly appreciate the term bulldog, which I had heard applied to him by the soldiers. Difficulties seem to make no other impression upon him than to make him a little more savage.

Major Walton was the only officer with him when I came up—all the rest had been put into the charge. In a few minutes Major Latrobe arrived on foot, carrying his saddle, having just had his horse killed. Colonel Sorrel was also in the same predicament, and Captain Goree's horse was wounded in the mouth.

The General was making the best arrangements in his power to resist the threatened advance, by advancing some

---

[45] For Longstreet's version of this meeting with Fremantle, see his *From Manassas to Appomattox: Memoirs of the Civil War in America* (Philadelphia: J. B. Lippincott, 1896), p. 394.

artillery, rallying the stragglers, &c. I remember seeing a General (Pettigrew, I think it was)* come up to him, and report that "he was unable to bring his men up again." Longstreet turned upon him and replied with some sarcasm: "*Very well; never mind, then, General; just let them remain where they are: the enemy's going to advance, and will spare you the trouble.*"

He asked for something to drink: I gave him some rum out of my silver flask, which I begged he would keep in remembrance of the occasion; he smiled, and, to my great satisfaction, accepted the memorial. He then went off to give some orders to McLaws's division. Soon afterwards I joined General Lee, who had in the mean while come to that part of the field on becoming aware of the disaster. If Longstreet's conduct was admirable, that of General Lee was perfectly sublime. He was engaged in rallying and in encouraging the broken troops, and was riding about a little in front of the wood, quite alone—the whole of his Staff being engaged in a similar manner further to the rear. His face, which is always placid and cheerful, did not show signs of the slightest disappointment, care, or annoyance; and he was addressing to every soldier he met a few words of encouragement, such as, "All this will come right in the end: we'll talk it over afterwards; but, in the mean time, all good men must rally. We want all good and true men just now," &c. He spoke to all the wounded men that passed him, and the slightly wounded he exhorted "to bind up their hurts and take up a musket" in this emergency. Very few failed to answer his appeal, and I saw many badly wounded men take off their hats and cheer him. He said to me, "This has been a sad day for us, Colonel—a sad day; but we can't expect always to gain victories." He was also kind enough to advise me to get into some more sheltered position, as the shells were bursting round us with considerable frequency.

Notwithstanding the misfortune which had so suddenly

---

*This officer was afterwards killed at the passage of the Potomac.

Brig. Gen. James Johnston Pettigrew

befallen him, General Lee seemed to observe every thing, however trivial. When a mounted officer began licking his horse for shying at the bursting of a shell, he called out, "Don't whip him, Captain; don't whip him. I've got just such another foolish horse myself, and whipping does no good."

I happened to see a man lying flat on his face in a small ditch, and I remarked that I didn't think he seemed dead; this drew General Lee's attention to the man, who commenced groaning dismally. Finding appeals to his patriotism of no avail, General Lee had him ignominiously set on his legs by some neighboring gunners.

I saw General Wilcox[46] (an officer who wears a short round jacket and a battered straw hat) come up to him, and explain, almost crying, the state of his brigade. General Lee immediately shook hands with him and said cheerfully, "Never mind, General, *all this has been* MY *fault*—it is *I* that have lost this fight, and you must help me out of it in the best way you can." In this manner I saw General Lee encourage and reanimate his somewhat dispirited troops, and magnanimously take upon his own shoulders the whole weight of the repulse. It was impossible to look at him or to listen to him without feeling the strongest admiration, and I never saw any man fail him except the man in the ditch.

It is difficult to exaggerate the critical state of affairs as they appeared about this time. If the enemy or their general had shown any enterprise, there is no saying what might have happened. General Lee and his officers were evidently fully impressed with a sense of the situation; yet there was much less noise, fuss, or confusion of orders than at an ordinary field-day; the men, as they were rallied in the wood, were brought up in detachments, and lay down quietly and coolly in the positions assigned to them.

---

[46] Brig. Gen. Cadmus Marcellus Wilcox, a native of North Carolina reared in Tennessee, commanded a brigade of Alabama troops in Maj. Gen. Richard H. Anderson's division of Hill's Third Corps.

We heard that Generals Garnett and Armistead were killed, and General Kemper mortally wounded;[47] also, that Pickett's division had only one field-officer unhurt. Nearly all this slaughter took place in an open space about one mile square, and within one hour.

At 6 P.M. we heard a long and continuous Yankee cheer, which we at first imagined was an indication of an advance; but it turned out to be their reception of a general officer, whom we saw riding down the line, followed by about thirty horsemen. Soon afterwards I rode to the extreme front, where there were four pieces of rifled cannon almost without any infantry support. To the non-withdrawal of these guns is to be attributed the otherwise surprising inactivity of the enemy. I was immediately surrounded by a sergeant and about half-a-dozen gunners, who seemed in excellent spirits and full of confidence, in spite of their exposed situation. The sergeant expressed his ardent hope that the Yankees might have spirit enough to advance and receive the dose he had in readiness for them. They spoke in admiration of the advance of Pickett's division, and of the manner in which Pickett himself had led it.[48] When they observed General Lee they said, "We've not lost confidence in the old man: this day's work won't do him no harm. 'Uncle Robert' will get us into Washington yet; you bet he will!" &c. Whilst we were talking, the enemy's skirmishers began to advance slowly, and several ominous sounds in quick succession told us that we were

[47] Brig. Gen. Lewis Addison Armistead, a native of North Carolina, Brig. Gen. Richard Brooke Garnett, a Virginian, and Brig. Gen. James Lawson Kemper, also of Virginia, each commanded one of the three brigades in Pickett's division. On July 3, Garnett was killed, Armistead mortally wounded, and Kemper severely wounded. Kemper subsequently became governor of his home state.

[48] Some Confederates questioned Pickett's courage after the assault, and his role on July 3 became the focus of a small contentious literature. For the best analysis of this question, see Kathleen R. Georg and John W. Busey, *Nothing But Glory: Pickett's Division at Gettysburg* (Hightstown, N.J.: Longstreet House, 1987), pp. 194–205.

Brig. Gen. Lewis Addison Armistead Just Before Receiving His Mortal Wound

attracting their attention, and that it was necessary to break up the conclave. I therefore turned round and took leave of these cheery and plucky gunners.

At 7 P.M., General Lee received a report that Johnson's division of Ewell's corps had been successful on the left, and had gained important advantages there. Firing entirely ceased in our front about this time; but we now heard some brisk musketry on our right, which I afterwards learned proceeded from Hood's Texans, who had managed to surround some enterprising Yankee cavalry, and were slaughtering them with great satisfaction. Only eighteen out of four hundred are said to have escaped.

At 7:30, all idea of a Yankee attack being over, I rode back to Moses's tent, and found that worthy commissary in very low spirits, all sorts of exaggerated rumors having reached him. On my way I met a great many wounded men, most anxious to inquire after Longstreet, who was reported killed; when I assured them he was quite well, they seemed to forget their own pain in the evident pleasure they felt in the safety of their chief. No words that I can use will adequately express the extraordinary patience and fortitude with which the wounded Confederates bore their sufferings.

I got something to eat with the doctors at 10 P.M., the first for fifteen hours.

I gave up my horse to-day to his owner, as from death and exhaustion the Staff are almost without horses.

4th July (Saturday).—I was awoke at daylight by Moses complaining that his valuable trunk, containing much public money, had been stolen from our tent whilst we slept. After a search it was found in a wood hard by, broken open and minus the money. Dr. Barksdale had been robbed in the same manner exactly. This is evidently the work of those rascally stragglers, who shirk going under fire, plunder the natives, and will hereafter swagger as the heroes of Gettysburg.

Lawley, the Austrian, and I, walked up to the front about eight o'clock, and on our way we met General Longstreet, who was in a high state of amusement and good humor. A flag of truce had just come over from the enemy, and its bearer announced among other things that "General Longstreet was wounded, and a prisoner, but would be taken care of." General Longstreet sent back word that he was extremely grateful, but that, being neither wounded nor a prisoner, he was quite able to take care of himself. The iron endurance of General Longstreet is most extraordinary: he seems to require neither food nor sleep. Most of his Staff now fall fast asleep directly they get off their horses, they are so exhausted from the last three days' work.

Whilst Lawley went to headquarters on business, I sat down and had a long talk with General Pendleton (the parson), chief of artillery. He told me the exact number of guns in action yesterday. He said that the universal opinion is in favor of the 12-pounder Napoleon guns as the best and simplest sort of ordnance for field purposes.* Nearly all the artillery with this army has either been captured from the enemy or cast from old 6-pounders taken at the early part of the war.

At 10 A.M. Lawley returned from headquarters, bringing the news that the army is to commence moving in the direction of Virginia this evening. This step is imperative from want of ammunition. But it was hoped that the enemy might attack during the day, especially as this is the 4th of July, and it was calculated that there was still ammunition for one day's fighting. The ordnance train had already commenced moving back towards Cashtown, and Ewell's immense train of plunder had been proceeding towards Hagerstown by the Fairfield road ever since an early hour this morning.

Johnson's division had evacuated during the night the position it had gained yesterday. It appears that for a time it

---

*The Napoleon 12-pounders are smooth-bore brass guns, with chambers, very light, and with long range. They were invented or recommended by Louis Napoleon years ago. A large number are being cast at Augusta and elsewhere.

was actually in possession of the cemetery, but had been forced to retire from thence from want of support by Pender's division, which had been retarded by that officer's wound. The whole of our left was therefore thrown back considerably.

At 1 P.M. the rain began to descend in torrents, and we took refuge in the hovel of an ignorant Pennsylvanian boor. The cottage was full of soldiers, none of whom had the slightest idea of the contemplated retreat, and all were talking of Washington and Baltimore with the greatest confidence.

At 2 P.M. we walked to General Longstreet's camp, which had been removed to a place three miles distant, on the Fairfield road. General Longstreet talked to me for a long time about the battle. He said the mistake they had made was in not concentrating the army more, and making the attack yesterday with 30,000 men instead of 15,000. The advance had been in three lines, and the troops of Hill's corps who gave way were young soldiers, who had never been under fire before. He thought the enemy would have attacked had the guns been withdrawn. Had they done so at that particular moment immediately after the repulse, it would have been awkward; but in that case he had given orders for the advance of Hood's division and McLaws's on the right. I think, after all, that General Meade was right not to advance—his men would never have stood the tremendous fire of artillery they would have been exposed to.

Rather over 7,000 Yankees were captured during the three days; 3,500 took the parole; the remainder were now being marched to Richmond, escorted by the remains of Pickett's division. It is impossible to avoid seeing that the cause of this check to the Confederates lies in the utter contempt felt for the enemy by all ranks.

Wagons, horses, mules, and cattle captured in Pennsylvania, the solid advantages of this campaign, have been passing slowly along this road (Fairfield) all day: those taken by Ewell are particularly admired. So interminable was this train that it soon became evident that we should not be able to

The Retreat from Gettysburg

start till late at night. As soon as it became dark we all lay round a big fire, and I heard reports coming in from the different generals that the enemy was *retiring,* and had been doing so all day long. McLaws reported nothing in his front but cavalry videttes. But this, of course, could make no difference to General Lee's plan: ammunition he must have—he had failed to capture it from the enemy (according to precedent); and as his communications with Virginia were intercepted, he was compelled to fall back towards Winchester, and draw his supplies from thence. General Milroy had kindly left an ample stock at that town when he made his precipitate exit some weeks ago. The army was also incumbered with an enormous wagon-train, the spoils of Pennsylvania, which it is highly desirable to get safely over the Potomac.

Shortly after 9 P.M. the rain began to descend in torrents. Lawley and I luckily got into the doctors' covered buggy, and began to get slowly under way a little after midnight.

5th July (Sunday).—The night was very bad—thunder and lightning, torrents of rain—the road knee-deep in mud and water, and often blocked up with wagons "come to grief." I pitied the wretched plight of the unfortunate soldiers who were to follow us. Our progress was naturally very slow indeed, and we took eight hours to go as many miles.

At 8 A.M. we halted a little beyond the village of Fairfield, near the entrance to a mountain-pass. No sooner had we done so, and lit a fire, than an alarm was spread that Yankee cavalry were upon us. Several shots flew over our heads, but we never could discover from whence they came. News also arrived of the capture of the whole of Ewell's beautiful wagons.* These reports created a regular stampede amongst the wagoners, and Longstreet's drivers started off as fast as they could go. Our medical trio, however, firmly declined to budge, and came to this wise conclusion, partly urged by the pangs of hunger, and partly from the consideration that, if

---

*It afterwards turned out that all escaped but thirty-eight.

the Yankee cavalry did come, the crowded state of the road in our rear would prevent our escape. Soon afterwards, some Confederate cavalry were pushed to the front, who cleared the pass after a slight skirmish.

At noon, Generals Lee and Longstreet arrived, and halted close to us. Soon afterwards Ewell came up. This is the first time I ever saw him. He is rather a remarkable-looking old soldier, with a bald head, a prominent nose, and rather a haggard, sickly face: having so lately lost his leg above the knee, he is still a complete cripple, and falls off his horse occasionally. Directly he dismounts he has to be put on crutches. He was Stonewall Jackson's coadjutor during the celebrated Valley campaigns, and he used to be a great swearer—in fact, he is said to have been the only person who was unable to restrain that propensity before Jackson; but since his late (rather romantic) marriage, he has (to use the American expression) *"joined the Church."* When I saw him he was in a great state of disgust in consequence of the supposed loss of his wagons, and refused to be comforted by General Lee.

I joined Longstreet again, and, mounted on Lawley's venerable horse, started at 3 P.M. to ride through the pass. At 4 P.M. we stopped at a place where the roads fork, one leading to Emmitsburg, and the other to Hagerstown. Major Moses and I entered a farm-house, in which we found several women, two wounded Yankees, and one dead one, the result of this morning's skirmish. One of the sufferers was frightfully wounded in the head; the other was hit in the knee: the latter told me he was an Irishman, and had served in the Bengal Europeans during the Indian Mutiny. He now belonged to a Michigan cavalry regiment, and had already imbibed American ideas of Ireland's wrongs, and all that sort of trash. He told me that his officers were very bad, and that the idea in the army was that McClellan had assumed the chief command.

The women in this house were great Abolitionists. When Major Fairfax rode up, he inquired of one of them whether the corpse was that of a Confederate or Yankee (the

Lt. Gen. Richard Stoddert Ewell

body was in the veranda, covered with a white sheet). The woman made a gesture with her foot, and replied, "If it was a rebel, do you think it would be here long?" Fairfax then said, "Is it a woman who speaks in such a manner of a dead body which can do no one any harm?" She thereupon colored up, and said she wasn't in earnest. At 6 o'clock we rode on again (by the Hagerstown road), and came up with General Longstreet at 7:30. The road was full of soldiers marching in a particularly lively manner—the wet and mud seemed to have produced no effect whatever on their spirits, which were as boisterous as ever. They had got hold of colored prints of Mr. Lincoln, which they were passing about from company to company with many remarks upon the personal beauty of Uncle Abe. The same old chaff was going on of "Come out of that hat—I know you're in it—I sees your legs a-dangling down," &c. When we halted for the night, skirmishing was going on in front and rear—Stuart in front and Ewell in rear. Our bivouac being near a large tavern, General Longstreet had ordered some supper there for himself and his Staff; but when we went to devour it, we discovered General McLaws and his officers rapidly finishing it. We, however, soon got more, the Pennsylvanian proprietors being particularly anxious to propitiate the General, in hopes that he would spare their live stock, which had been condemned to death by the ruthless Moses.

During supper, women came rushing in at intervals, saying—"Oh, good heavens, now they're killing our fat hogs. Which is the General? which is the Great Officer? Our milch cows are now going." To all which expressions Longstreet replied, shaking his head in a melancholy manner—"Yes, madam, it's very sad—very sad; and this sort of thing has been going on in Virginia more than two years—very sad." We all slept in the open, and the heavy rain produced no effect upon our slumbers.

I understand it is impossible to cross the lines by flag of truce. I therefore find myself in a dilemma about the expiration of my leave.

6th July (Monday).—Several horses were stolen last night, mine nearly so. It is necessary to be very careful, in order to prevent this misfortune. We started at 6:30, but got on very slowly, so blocked up was the road with wagons, some of which had been captured and burnt by the enemy yesterday. It now turned out that all Ewell's wagons escaped except thirty-eight, although, at one time, they had been all in the enemy's hands.

At 8:30 we halted for a couple of hours, and Generals Lee, Longstreet, Hill, and Wilcox, had a consultation. I spoke to —— about my difficulties with regard to getting home, and the necessity of doing so, owing to the approaching expiration of my leave. He told me that the army had no intention at present of retreating for good, and advised me to stop with them and see what turned up. He also said that some of the enemy's dispatches had been intercepted, in which the following words occur:—"The noble but unfortunate army of the Potomac has again been obliged to retreat before superior numbers." I particularly observed the marching to-day of the 21st Mississippi, which was uncommonly good. This regiment all wear short round jackets, a most unusual circumstance, for they are generally unpopular in the South.

At 12 o'clock we halted again, and all set to work to eat cherries, which was the only food we got between 5 A.M. and 11 P.M.

I saw a most laughable spectacle this afternoon—viz., a negro dressed in full Yankee uniform, with a rifle at full cock, leading along a barefooted white man, with whom he had evidently changed clothes. General Longstreet stopped the pair, and asked the black man what it meant. He replied, "The two soldiers in charge of this here Yank have got drunk, so for fear he should escape I have took care of him, and brought him through that little town." The consequential manner of the negro, and the supreme contempt with which he spoke to his prisoner, were most amusing. This little episode of a Southern slave leading a white Yankee soldier through a Northern village, *alone and of his own accord,* would not have been gratifying to an abolitionist. Nor would the sympathizers both in England and in the North feel encouraged if they could hear the language of detestation and contempt with which the numerous negroes with the Southern armies speak of their liberators.*

I saw General Hood in his carriage; he looked rather bad, and has been suffering a good deal; the doctors seem to doubt whether they will be able to save his arm. I also saw General Hampton,[49] of the cavalry, who has been shot in the hip, and has two sabre-cuts on the head, but he was in very good spirits.

A short time before we reached Hagerstown there was some firing in front, together with an alarm that the Yankee cavalry was upon us. The ambulances were sent back; but some of the wounded jumped out, and, producing the rifles

---

*From what I have seen of the Southern negroes, I am of opinion that the Confederates could, if they chose, convert a great number into soldiers; and from the affection which undoubtedly exists as a general rule between the slaves and their masters, I think that they would prove more efficient than black troops under any other circumstances. But I do not imagine that such an experiment will be tried, except as a very last resort, partly on account of the great value of the negroes, and partly because the Southerners consider it improper to introduce such an element on a large scale into civilized warfare. Any person who has seen negro features convulsed with rage, may form a slight estimate of what the result would be of arming a vast number of blacks, rousing their passions, and then allowing them free scope.[50]

[49] Brig. Gen. Wade Hampton, a wealthy South Carolina planter who commanded a brigade of Confederate cavalry, was severely wounded during the cavalry battle east of Gettysburg on July 3.

[50] When Confederate political and military leaders eventually did confront the question of arming black men, it was too late to have a significant impact on the course of the war. See Robert F. Durden, *The Gray and the Black: The Confederate Debate on Emancipation* (Baton Rouge, La.: Louisiana State University Press, 1972). Fremantle's obvious prejudice caused him to doubt the ability of black soldiers to achieve the discipline necessary to succeed as soldiers, but the nearly 200,000 black men who served in the Union army provided crucial support to the northern war effort at a time when white enlistments were lagging and proved their mettle on many battlefields.

which they had not parted with, they prepared to fight. After a good deal of desultory skirmishing, we seated ourselves upon a hill overlooking Hagerstown, and saw the enemy's cavalry driven through the town pursued by yelling Confederates. A good many Yankee prisoners now passed us; one of them who was smoking a cigar, was a lieutenant of cavalry, dressed very smartly, and his hair brushed with the greatest care; he formed rather a contrast to his ragged escort, and to ourselves, who had not washed or shaved for ever so long.

About 7 P.M. we rode through Hagerstown, in the streets of which were several dead horses and a few dead men. After proceeding about a mile beyond the town we halted, and General Longstreet sent four cavalrymen up a lane, with directions to report every thing they saw. We then dismounted and lay down. About ten minutes later (being nearly dark) we heard a sudden rush—a panic—and then a regular stampede commenced, in the midst of which I descried our four cavalry heroes crossing a field as fast as they could gallop. All was now complete confusion;—officers mounting their horses, and pursuing those which had got loose, and soldiers climbing over fences for protection against the supposed advancing Yankees. In the middle of the din I heard an artillery officer shouting to his "cannoneers" to stand by him, and plant the guns in a proper position for enfilading the lane. I also distinguished Longstreet walking about, hustled by the excited crowd, and remarking, in angry tones, which could scarcely be heard, and to which no attention was paid, "Now, you don't know what it is—you don't know what it is." Whilst the row and confusion were at their height, the object of all this alarm at length emerged from the dark lane, in the shape of a domestic four-wheel carriage, with a harmless load of females. The stampede had, however, spread, increased in the rear, and caused much harm and delay.

Cavalry skirmishing went on until quite dark, a determined attack having been made by the enemy, who did his best to prevent the trains from crossing the Potomac at Williamsport. It resulted in the success of the Confederates; but every impartial man confesses that these cavalry fights are miserable affairs. Neither party has any idea of serious charging with the sabre. They approach one another with considerable boldness, until they get to within about forty yards, and then, at the very moment when a dash is necessary, and the sword alone should be used, they hesitate, halt, and commence a desultory fire with carbines and revolvers. An Englishman, named Winthrop, a captain in the Confederate army, and formerly an officer in H.M.'s 22d regiment, although not in the cavalry himself, seized the colors of one of the regiments, and rode straight at the Yankees in the most gallant manner, shouting to the men to follow him. He continued to distinguish himself by leading charges until his horse was unfortunately killed. I heard his conduct on this occasion highly spoken of by all.[51] Stuart's cavalry can hardly be called cavalry in the European sense of the word; but, on the other hand, the country in which they are accustomed to operate is not adapted for cavalry.

——— was forced at last to give up wearing even his Austrian forage-cap; for the last two days soldiers on the line of march had been visiting his ambulance in great numbers, under the impression (encouraged by the driver) that he was a Yankee general. The idea now was that the army would remain some days in or near its present position until the arrival of the ammunition from Winchester.

7th July (Tuesday).—Lawley, the Austrian, and I drove into Hagerstown this morning, and General Longstreet

[51] Capt. Stephen Winthrop had just joined the staff of Col. E. P. Alexander, who described him as "good natured, jolly, & brave. . . . He was an excellent and admirable representation of his country, & proved in every way an agreeable accession to our mess. . . ." Alexander did note a somewhat troubling "peculiarity" of Winthrop's character—"his fondness for killing things. It was not cruelty—that is he did not go out to kill things unnecessarily—but destructiveness! If anything had to be killed he loved to do it." Alexander, *Fighting for the Confederacy*, p. 268.

moved into a new position on the Williamsport road, which he was to occupy for the present. We got an excellent room in the Washington Hotel on producing greenbacks. Public opinion in Hagerstown seems to be pretty evenly divided between North and South, and probably accommodates itself to circumstances. For instance, yesterday the women waved their handkerchiefs when the Yankee cavalry were driven through the town, and to-day they went through the same compliment in honor of 3,500 Yankee (Gettysburg) prisoners whom I saw march through *en route* for Richmond. I over-heard the conversation of some Confederate soldiers about these prisoners. One remarked, with respect to the Zouaves, of whom there were a few—"Those red-breeched fellows look as if they could fight, but they don't, though; no, not so well as the blue-bellies."

Lawley introduced me to General Stuart in the streets of Hagerstown to-day. He is commonly called Jeb Stuart, on account of his initials; he is a good-looking, jovial character, exactly like his photographs. He has certainly accomplished wonders, and done excellent service in his peculiar style of warfare. He is a good and gallant soldier, though he some-times incurs ridicule by his harmless affectation and peculiar-ities. The other day he rode through a Virginian town, his horse covered with garlands of roses. He also departs consid-erably from the severe simplicity of dress adopted by other Confederate generals; but no one can deny that he is the right man in the right place. On a campaign, he seems to roam over the country according to his own discretion, and always gives a good account of himself, turning up at the right moment; and hitherto he has never got himself into any serious trouble.[52]

---

[52] Stuart's poor judgment early in the campaign left Lee groping blindly in Maryland and Pennsylvania, inviting severe censure at the time and from historians since. Although officially silent during the war about his unhappiness with Stuart's performance between mid-June and July 2, 1863, Lee commented after the war that the cavalryman's "failure to carry out his instructions *forced the battle of Gettysburg*."

I rode to General Longstreet's camp, which is about two miles in the direction of Williamsport, and consulted him about my difficulties with regard to my leave. He was most good-natured about it, and advised me under the circumstances to drive in the direction of Hancock; and in the event of being ill-treated on the way, to insist upon being taken before the nearest U.S. officer of the highest rank, who would probably protect me. I determined to take his advice at once; so I took leave of him and of his officers. Longstreet is generally a very taciturn and undemonstrative man, but he was quite affectionate in his farewell. His last words were a hearty hope for the speedy termination of the war. All his officers were equally kind in their expressions on my taking leave, though the last sentence uttered by Latrobe was not entirely reassuring—viz., "You may take your oath he'll be caught for a spy."

I then rode to General Lee's camp, and asked him for a pass to get through his lines. We had a long talk together, and he told me of the raid made by the enemy, for the express purpose of arresting his badly wounded son (a Confederate Brigadier-general), who was lying in the house of a relation in Virginia. They insisted upon carrying him off in a litter, though he had never been out of bed, and had quite recently been shot through the thigh. This seizure was evidently made for purposes of retaliation. His life has since been threatened, in the event of the South retaliating for Burnside's alleged military murders in Kentucky.[53]

But few officers, however, speak of the Northerners with so much moderation as General Lee; his extreme amiability seems to prevent his speaking strongly against any one.

[53] Brig. Gen. William Henry Fitzhugh "Rooney" Lee, the general's second son, had been wounded on June 9, 1863, at the battle of Brandy Station. He remained in Federal hands until March 1864. Maj. Gen. Ambrose Everett Burnside, a native of Indiana who commanded the Department of Ohio, had taken strong measures against disloyal citizens— including Clement L. Vallandigham, who was arrested on Burnside's orders.

Maj. Gen. James Ewell Brown Stuart

I really felt quite sorry when I said good-by to so many gentlemen from whom I had received so much disinterested kindness.

I am now about to leave the Southern States, after travelling quite alone throughout their entire length and breadth, including Texas and the trans-Mississippi country, for nearly three months and a half, during which time I have been thrown amongst all classes of the population—the highest and lowest, and the most lawless. Although many were very sore about the conduct of England, I never received an uncivil word from anybody, but, on the contrary, I have been treated by all with more than kindness.* I have never met a man who was not anxious for a termination of the war; and I have never met a man, woman, or child who contemplated its termination as possible without an entire separation from the *now* detested Yankee. I have never been asked for alms or a gratuity by any man or woman, black or white. Every one knew who I was, and all spoke to me with the greatest confidence. I have rarely heard any person complain of the almost total ruin which had befallen so many. All are prepared to undergo still greater sacrifices,—they contemplate and prepare to receive greater reverses which it is impossible to avert. They look to a successful termination of the war as certain, although few are sanguine enough to fix a speedy date for it, and nearly all bargain for its lasting at least all Lincoln's presidency. Although I have always been with the Confederates in the time of their misfortunes, yet I never heard any person use a desponding word as to the result of the struggle. When I was in Texas and Louisiana, Banks seemed to be carrying every thing before him, Grant[54] was doing the same in Missis-

*The only occasion on which I was roughly handled was when I had the misfortune to enter the city of Jackson, Mississippi, just as the Federals evacuated it. I do not complain of that affair, which, under the circumstances, was not to be wondered at.

[54] At the time Fremantle traveled in Texas and Louisiana, a Union army under Maj. Gen. Ulysses S. Grant of Ohio was investing the Confederate stronghold of Vicksburg, Mississippi. Vicksburg capitulated on July 4, 1863.

sippi, and I certainly did not bring luck to my friends at Gettysburg. I have lived in bivouacs with all the Southern armies, which are as distinct from one another as the British is from the Austrian, and I have never once seen an instance of insubordination.

When I got back to Hagerstown, I endeavored to make arrangements for a horse and buggy to drive through the lines. With immense difficulty I secured the services of a Mr. ——, to take me to Hancock, and as much further as I chose to go, for a dollar a mile (greenbacks). I engaged also to pay him the value of his horse and buggy, in case they should be confiscated by either side. He was evidently extremely alarmed, and I was obliged to keep him up to the mark by assurances that his horse would inevitably be seized by the Confederates, unless protected by General Lee's pass in my possession.

8th July (Wednesday).—My conductor told me he couldn't go to-day on account of a funeral, but he promised faithfully to start to-morrow. Every one was full of forebodings as to my probable fate when I fell into Yankee clutches. In deference to their advice I took off my gray shooting-jacket, in which they said I was sure to be taken for a rebel, and I put on a black coat; but I scouted all well-meant advice as to endeavoring to disguise myself as an "American citizen," or to conceal the exact truth in any way. I was aware that a great deal depended upon falling into the hands of a gentleman, and I did not believe these were so rare in the Northern army as the Confederates led me to suppose.

9th July (Thursday).—I left Hagerstown at 8 A.M., in my conductor's good buggy, after saying farewell to Lawley, the Austrian, and the numerous Confederate officers who came to see me off, and wish me good-luck. We passed the Confederate advanced post at about two miles from Hagerstown, and were allowed to pass on the production of General Lee's authority. I was now fairly launched beyond the Confederate lines for the first time since I had been in America.

Immediately afterwards we began to be asked all sorts of inquisitive questions about the rebels, which I left to my driver to answer. It became perfectly evident that this narrow strip of Maryland is entirely Unionist.

At about 12 o'clock we reached the top of a high hill, and halted to bait our horse at an inn called Fairview. No sooner had we descended from the buggy than about twenty rampageous Unionists appeared, who told us they had come up to get a good view of the big fight in which the G—d d—d rebels were to be all captured, or drowned in the Potomac. My appearance evidently did not please them from the very first. With alarm I observed them talking to one another, and pointing at me. At length a particularly truculent-looking individual, with an enormous mustache, approached me, and, fixing his eyes long and steadfastly upon my trousers, he remarked, in the surliest possible tones, *"Them breeches is a d—d bad color."* This he said in allusion, not to their dirty state, but to the fact of their being gray, the rebel color. I replied to this very disagreeable assertion in as conciliating a way as I possibly could; and in answer to his question as to who I was, I said that I was an English traveller. He then said that his wife was an English lady from Preston. I next expressed my pride of being a countryman of his wife's. He then told me in tones that admitted of no contradiction, that Preston was just forty-five miles east of London; and he afterwards launched into torrents of invectives against the rebels, who had *run him* out of Virginia; and he stated his intention of killing them in great numbers to gratify his taste. With some difficulty I prevailed upon him and his rabid brethren to drink, which pacified them slightly for a time; but when the horse was brought out to be harnessed, it became evident I was not to be allowed to proceed without a row. I therefore addressed the crowd, and asked them quietly who among them wished to detain me; and I told them at the same time, that I would not answer any questions put by those who were not persons in authority, but that I should be most happy to explain myself to any officer of the United States army. At length they allowed me to proceed, on the understanding that my buggy-driver should hand me over to General Kelley,[55] at Hancock. The driver was provided with a letter for the general, in which I afterwards discovered that I was denounced as a spy, and "handed over to the General *to be dealt with as justice to our cause demands.*" We were then allowed to start, the driver being threatened with condign vengeance if he let me escape.

After we had proceeded about six miles we fell in with some Yankee cavalry, by whom we were immediately captured, and the responsibility of my custody was thus removed from my conductor's shoulders. A cavalry soldier was put in charge of us, and we passed through the numerous Yankee outposts under the title of *"Prisoners."*

The hills near Hancock were white with Yankee tents, and there were, I believe, from 8,000 to 10,000 Federals there. I did not think much of the appearance of the Northern troops; they are certainly dressed in proper uniform, but their clothes are badly fitted, and they are often round-shouldered, dirty, and slovenly in appearance; in fact, bad imitations of soldiers. Now, the Confederate has no ambition to imitate the regular soldier at all; he looks the genuine rebel; but in spite of his bare feet, his ragged clothes, his old rug, and tooth-brush stuck like a rose in his button-hole,* he has a sort of devil-may-care, reckless, self-confident look, which is decidedly taking.

At 5 P.M. we drove up in front of the door of General Kelley's quarters, and to my immense relief I soon discovered that he was a gentleman. I then explained to him the whole truth, concealing nothing. I said I was a British officer on leave of absence, travelling for my own instruction; that I had

---

*This tooth-brush in the button-hole is a very common custom, and has a most quaint effect.

[55] Brig. Gen. Benjamin Franklin Kelley, a native of New Hampshire who as a young man had moved to Wheeling, Virginia (now West Virginia), commanded Union troops charged with protecting the Baltimore and Ohio Railroad.

Brig. Gen. Benjamin Franklin Kelley

been all the way to Mexico, and entered the Southern States by the Rio Grande, for the express purpose of not breaking any legally established blockade. I told him I had visited all the Southern armies in Mississippi, Tennessee, Charleston, and Virginia, and seen the late campaign as General Long-street's guest, but had in no way entered the Confederate service. I also gave him my word that I had not got in my possession any letters, either public or private, from any person in the South to any person anywhere else. I showed him my British passport and General Lee's pass as a British officer; and I explained that my only object in coming North was to return to England in time for the expiration of my leave; and I ended by expressing a hope that he would make my detention as short as possible.

After considering a short time, he said that he would certainly allow me to go on, but that he could not allow my driver to go back. I felt immensely relieved at the decision, but the countenance of my companion lengthened considerably. It was, however, settled that he should take me on to Cumberland, and General Kelley good-naturedly promised to do what he could for him on his return.

General Kelley then asked me in an off-hand manner whether all General Lee's army was at Hagerstown; but I replied, laughing, "You of course understand, General, that, having got that pass from General Lee, I am bound by every principle of honor not to give you any information which can be of advantage to you." He laughed and promised not to ask me any more questions of that sort. He then sent his aid-de-camp with me to the provost-marshal, who immediately gave me a pass for Cumberland. On my return to the General's, I discovered the perfidious driver (that zealous Southerner a few hours previous) hard at work communicating to General Kelley all he knew, and a great deal more besides; but, from what I heard, I don't think his information was very valuable.

I was treated by General Kelley and all his officers with the greatest good-nature and courtesy, although I had certainly come among them under circumstances suspicious, to say the least. I felt quite sorry that they should be opposed to my Southern friends, and I regretted still more that they should be obliged to serve with or under a Butler, a Milroy, or even a Hooker. I took leave of them at six o'clock; and I can truly say that the only Federal officers I have ever come in contact with were gentlemen.

We had got four miles beyond Hancock, when the tire of one of our wheels came off, and we had to stop for a night at a farm-house. I had supper with the farmer and his laborers, who had just come in from the fields, and the supper was much superior to that which can be procured at the first hotel at Richmond. All were violent Unionists, and perfectly under the impression that the rebels were totally demoralized, and about to lay down their arms. Of course I held my tongue, and gave no one reason to suppose that I had ever been in rebeldom.

10th July (Friday).—The drive from Hancock to Cumberland is a very mountainous forty-four miles—total distance from Hagerstown, sixty-six miles. We met with no further adventure on the road, although the people were very inquisitive, but I never opened my mouth. One woman in particular, who kept a toll-bar, thrust her ugly old head out of an upper window, and yelled out, "Air they a-fixin' for another battle out there?" jerking her head in the direction of Hagerstown. The driver replied that, although the bunch of rebels there was pretty big, yet he could not answer for their fixing arrangements, which he afterwards explained to me meant digging fortifications.

We arrived at Cumberland at 7 P.M. This is a great coal place, and a few weeks ago it was touched up by "Imboden,"[56] who burnt a lot of coal barges, which has rendered the people rabid against the Rebs. I started by stage for Johnstown at 8:30 P.M.

[56] Fremantle's reference is to a raid into northwestern Virginia in late spring 1863 carried out by troops under Brig. Gen. John D. Imboden and Brig. Gen. William E. "Grumble" Jones, both of Virginia.

11th July (Saturday).—I hope I may never for my sins be again condemned to travel for thirty hours in an American stage on a used-up plank-road. We changed carriages at Somerset. All my fellow-travellers were of course violent Unionists, and invariably spoke of my late friends as Rebels or Rebs. They had all got into their heads that their Potomac army, not having been thoroughly thrashed, as it always has been hitherto, had achieved a tremendous victory; and that its new chief, General Meade, who in reality was driven into a strong position, which he had sense enough to stick to, is a wonderful strategist. They all hope that the remnants of Lee's army will not be allowed to ESCAPE over the Potomac; whereas, when I left the army two days ago, no man in it had a thought of escaping over the Potomac, and certainly General Meade was not in a position to attempt to prevent the passage, if crossing had become necessary.

I reached Johnstown on the Pennsylvania Railway at 6 P.M., and found that town in a great state of excitement in consequence of the review of two militia companies, who were receiving garlands from the fair ladies of Johnstown in gratitude for their daring conduct in turning out to resist Lee's invasion. Most of the men seemed to be respectable mechanics, not at all adapted for an early interview with the rebels. The garlands supplied were as big and apparently as substantial as a ship's life-buoys, and the recipients looked particularly helpless after they had got them. Heaven help those Pennsylvanian braves if a score of Hood's Texans had caught sight of them![57]

---

[57] Fremantle captured the contempt veteran Confederate soldiers held for militia troops. In speaking of a brush with the 26th Pennsylvania Militia prior to the battle of Gettysburg, Confederate Maj. Gen. Jubal A. Early observed: "This was a part of Governor Curtin's contingent for the defence of the State, and seemed to belong to that class of men who regard 'discretion as the better part of valor.' It was well that the regiment took to its heels so quickly, or some of its members might have been hurt, and all would have been captured." Jubal A. Early, *Lieutenant General Jubal Anderson Early, C.S.A.: Autobiographical Sketch and Narrative of the War Between the States* (Philadelphia: J. B. Lippincott, 1912), pp. 257–58.

Left Johnstown by train at 7:30 P.M., and by paying half a dollar, I secured a berth in a sleeping-car—a most admirable and ingenious Yankee notion.

12th July (Sunday).—The Pittsburgh and Philadelphia Railway is, I believe, accounted one of the best in America, which did not prevent my spending eight hours last night off the line; but, being asleep at the time, I was unaware of the circumstance. Instead of arriving at Philadelphia at 6 A.M., we did not get there till 3 P.M. Passed Harrisburg at 9 A.M. It was full of Yankee soldiers, and has evidently not recovered from the excitement consequent upon the late invasion, one effect of which has been to prevent the cutting of the crops by the calling out of the militia.

At Philadelphia I saw a train containing one hundred and fifty Confederate prisoners, who were being stared at by a large number of the *beau monde* of Philadelphia. I mingled with the crowd which was chaffing them. Most of the people were good-natured, but I heard one suggestion to the effect that they should be taken to the river, "and every mother's son of them drowned there."

I arrived at New York at 10 P.M., and drove to the Fifth Avenue Hotel.

13th July (Monday).—The luxury and comfort of New York and Philadelphia strike one as extraordinary after having lately come from Charleston and Richmond. The greenbacks seem to be nearly as good as gold. The streets are as full as possible of well-dressed people, and are crowded with able-bodied civilians capable of bearing arms, who have evidently no intention of doing so. They apparently *don't feel the war at all* here; and until there is a grand smash with their money, or some other catastrophe to make them feel it, I can easily imagine that they will not be anxious to make peace.

I walked the whole distance of Broadway to the Consul's house, and nothing could exceed the apparent prosperity; the street was covered with banners and placards inviting people to enlist in various high-sounding regiments. Bounties of $550 were offered, and huge pictures hung across the street, on which numbers of ragged *Graybacks,** terror depicted on their features, were being pursued by the Federals.

On returning to the Fifth Avenue, I found all the shopkeepers beginning to close their stores, and I perceived by degrees that there was great alarm about the resistance to the draft which was going on this morning. On reaching the hotel I perceived a whole block of buildings on fire close by: engines were present, but were not allowed to play by the crowd. In the hotel itself, universal consternation prevailed, and an attack by the mob had been threatened. I walked about in the neighborhood, and saw a company of soldiers on the march, who were being jeered at and hooted by small boys, and I saw a negro pursued by the crowd take refuge with the military; he was followed by loud cries of "Down with the b—y nigger! Kill all niggers!" &c. Never having been in New York before, and being totally ignorant of the state of feeling with regard to negroes, I inquired of a by-stander what the negroes had done that they should want to kill them? He replied civilly enough—"Oh sir, they hate them here; they are the innocent cause of all these troubles."[58]

Shortly afterwards, I saw a troop of citizen cavalry come up; the troopers were very gorgeously attired, but evidently expe-

---

*The Northerners call the Southerners "Graybacks," just as the latter call the former "Bluebellies," on account of the color of their dress.

[58] On the draft riots in New York City, which gave vent to hostility to black people across much of the North, see Adrian Cook, *The Armies of the Streets: The New York City Draft Riots of 1863* (Lexington, Ky.: The University Press of Kentucky, 1974), which provides a good narrative, and Iver Bernstein, *The New York City Draft Riots: Their Significance for American Society and Politics in the Age of the Civil War* (New York: Oxford University Press, 1990), which takes a more analytical approach to the subject.

rienced so much difficulty in sitting their horses, that they were more likely to excite laughter than any other emotion.

14th July (Tuesday).—At breakfast this morning two Irish waiters, seeing I was a Britisher, came up to me one after another, and whispered at intervals in hoarse Hibernian accents—"It's disgraceful, sir. I've been drafted, sir. I'm a Briton. I love my country. I love the Union Jack, sir." I suggested an interview with Mr. Archibald,[59] but neither of them seemed to care about going to the *Counsel* just yet. These rascals have probably been hard at work for years, voting as free and enlightened American citizens, and abusing England to their hearts' content.

I heard every one talking of the total demoralization of the Rebels as a certain fact, and all seemed to anticipate their approaching destruction. All this sounded very absurd to me, who had left Lee's army four days previously as full of fight as ever—much stronger in numbers, and ten times more efficient in every military point of view, than it was *when it crossed the Potomac to invade Maryland a year ago.* In its own opinion, Lee's army has not lost any of its prestige at the battle of Gettysburg, in which it most gallantly stormed strong intrenchments defended by the whole army of the Potomac, which never ventured outside its works, or approached in force within half a mile of the Confederate artillery.[60]

The result of the battle of Gettysburg, together with the fall of Vicksburg and Port Hudson, seems to have turned everybody's head completely, and has deluded them with the

---

[59] E. M. Archibald, who since 1857 had been British Consul-General in New York.

[60] On the question of the impact of Gettysburg on Lee's army and the rest of the Confederacy, see Gary W. Gallagher, " 'Lee's Army Has Not Lost Any of Its Prestige': The Impact of Gettysburg on the Army of Northern Virginia and the Confederate Home Front," in Gary W. Gallagher, ed., *The Third Day at Gettysburg and Beyond* (Chapel Hill, N.C.: University of North Carolina Press, 1994).

Scene from the New York City Draft Riots

idea of the speedy and complete subjugation of the South. I was filled with astonishment to hear the people speaking in this confident manner, when one of their most prosperous States had been so recently laid under contribution as far as Harrisburg; and Washington, their capital itself, having just been saved by a fortunate turn of luck. Four-fifths of the Pennsylvanian spoil had safely crossed the Potomac before I left Hagerstown.

The consternation in the streets seemed to be on the increase; fires were going on in all directions, and the streets were being patrolled by large bodies of police followed by special constables, the latter bearing truncheons, but not looking very happy. I heard a British captain making a deposition before the Consul, to the effect that the mob had got on board his vessel, and cruelly beaten his colored crew. As no British man-of-war was present, the French Admiral was appealed to, who at once requested that all British ships with colored crews might be anchored under the guns of his frigate.

The reports of outrages, hangings, and murder, were now most alarming, the terror and anxiety were universal. All shops were shut: all carriages and omnibuses had ceased running. No colored man or woman was visible or safe in the streets, or even in his own dwelling. Telegraphs were cut, and railroad tracks torn up. The draft was suspended, and the mob evidently had the upper hand.

The people who can't pay $300 naturally hate being forced to fight in order to liberate the very race who they are most anxious should be slaves. It is their direct interest not only that all slaves should remain slaves, but that the free Northern negroes who compete with them for labor should be sent to the South also.

15th July (Wednesday).—The hotel this morning was occupied by military, or rather by creatures in uniform. One of the sentries stopped me; and on my remonstrating to his officer, the latter blew up the sentry, and said, "You are only to stop persons in military dress—don't you know what military dress is?" "No," responded this efficient sentry—and I left the pair discussing the definition of a soldier. I had the greatest difficulty in getting a conveyance down to the water.

I saw a stone barricade in the distance, and heard firing going on—and I was not at all sorry to find myself on board the China.

Appendix

The Structure of the Armies

By the time of Gettysburg, Union and Confederate armies shared a similiar type of organization. Each was divided into corps. The seven infantry corps in the Army of the Potomac mustered an average of just more than 11,000 men each; the three infantry corps in the Army of Northern Virginia averaged just more than 21,000 men each. The Union army's Cavalry Corps counted almost 12,000 troopers, while the Cavalry Division in the Army of Northern Virginia (Lee's cavalry would be organized as a corps after Gettysburg) numbered about 7,000 troopers.

Each corps was divided into divisions. In Meade's army, the First, Second, Fifth, Sixth, and Eleventh corps each had three divisions; the Third and Twelfth corps two divisions apiece. In Lee's army, all three infantry corps had three divisions. The Union infantry divisions averaged roughly 3,800 men each; the Confederate infantry divisions about 6,500 men each.

Two or more brigades made up each of the infantry divisions in the Army of the Potomac, with 51 brigades total. In the Army of Northern Virginia, the nine infantry divisions contained a total of 37 brigades.

The basic unit of organization in each army was the regiment. Union infantry brigades averaged 4–5 regiments each, and the army contained 238 infantry regiments altogether. In Lee's army, the 37 brigades mustered 170 regiments. By regulation, a regiment consisted of ten companies of 100 men each, for a strength on paper of 1,000. But battle casualties and loss to disease had reduced the average regimental strength at Gettysburg to just more than 300 men in the Union army and slightly fewer than 340 men in the Confederate army.

The Army of the Potomac's Cavalry Corps consisted of three divisions further divided into 7 brigades and 29 regiments, with the average regimental strength just fewer than 360. The Cavalry Division in Lee's army mustered five brigades divided into 22 regiments, with an average regimental strength of almost 280 troopers.

The basic unit for artillery on each side was the battery. Union batteries normally had six cannon; the typical Confederate battery counted just four guns. Batteries were grouped into brigades in the Union army; each infantry corps had one artillery brigade made up of five batteries (the brigade in the Twelfth Corps had just four batteries), the Cavalry had two brigades of horse artillery, and the army as a whole had an artillery reserve of five brigades. Batteries were grouped into battalions in the Confederate army; each division had one battalion made up of four batteries (the battalion attached to R. H. Anderson's division had just 3 batteries), the Cavalry Division had six batteries of horse artillery, and each infantry corps had an artillery reserve of two battalions. Overall, the Army of the Potomac had 65 batteries totaling 358 cannon engaged at Gettysburg, while the Army of Northern Virginia had 67 batteries totaling 266 guns.

A word about ranks also is in order. The Union army had just two grades of general officers: the higher rank was major general, held by army commanders, corps commanders, and some division commanders; brigadier generals in the Union army commanded either divisions or brigades. The Confederate army had four grades of general officers: generals commanded armies; lieutenant generals commanded corps; major generals commanded divisions; and brigadier generals commanded brigades. The chief artillery officer in each army held the rank of brigadier general. In both armies, regiments usually were led by colonels.

Index